CHAUCER'S
THE CANTERBURY TALES

CONTINUUM READER'S GUIDES

CHAUCER'S
THE CANTERBURY TALES

GAIL ASHTON

continuum

Continuum
The Tower Building
11 York Road
London
SE1 7NX

80 Maiden Lane
Suite 704
New York
NY 10038

British Library Cataloguing-in-Publication Data
A catalogue record for this book is available from the British Library.

ISBN: HB: 0-8264-8935-4
978-08264-8935-7
PB: 0-8264-8936-2
978-08264-8936-4

Library of Congress Cataloging-in-Publication Data
Ashton, Gail, 1957–
Chaucer's The Canterbury tales / Gail Ashton.
p. cm.
Includes bibliographical references and index.
ISBN-13: 978-0-8264-8935-7
ISBN-10: 0-8264-8935-4
ISBN-13: 978-0-8264-8936-4
ISBN-10: 0-8264-8936-2
1. Chaucer, Geoffrey, d. 1400. Canterbury tales. 2. Tales, Medieval—
History and criticism. I. Title.

PR1874.A84 2007
821'.1—dc22

2007002769

Typeset by Servis Filmsetting Ltd, Manchester
Printed and bound in Great Britain by
Cromwell Press, Trowbridge, Wilts

CONTENTS

v

All references are to Larry D. Benson ed. (1988), *The Riverside Chaucer*, 3rd edition by Houghton Mifflin Company.

CHAPTER 1

CONTEXTS

CHAUCER'S LIFE

The survival of legal documents and civic records tells us much about Geoffrey Chaucer's career as a wily royal servant and about his circle of influential friends. Recent scholarly findings also help us to speculate about his possible political inclinations. But hardly any historical or social referents point us towards his private life or, perhaps surprisingly, his literary endeavours. It seems Chaucer was not especially reputed in his lifetime as a writer any more than we can track a definite image of him as a man. Is Chaucer the self-effacing 'popet' described by the Host in *The Canterbury Tales* (VII, 701)? Or the anxious man of the *Retraction* who recants all sinful works, in other words most of his poetry? Perhaps he is the unworldly narrator of the *Legend of Good Women*, dashing from his books to admire the daisies in the garden? If so, how does this square with the 'public' man known from the life records: the Justice of the Peace, the civil servant, diplomat, and possible rapist? When so few facts remain to us, we might even ask why examine Chaucer's biography at all? Yet this patchy archive underpins the ways in which we construct, and then interpret, versions of the figure we know as 'Chaucer'. It doesn't necessarily illuminate his writing or reveal how text and life marry (they don't). But it does help us respond critically to the 'Chaucer' who circulates in both medieval and more contemporary cultures.

This process began when the first biographies of Chaucer appeared in the sixteenth century from compilers such as Thomas

Speght, who prefaced his 'Chaucer collection' with a brief outline of the man's life. These early sources tend to repeat popular ideas rather than refer to historical sources. Speght, for example, recounts how Chaucer was fined for beating a Franciscan friar, an anecdote springing from an English-Protestant reading of Chaucer as an anti-Church satirist. Yet this competes with the fact that as a JP, Chaucer was required to uphold rather than break the law. Some modern biographers still take a distinctive stance in their interpretation of Chaucer's life records. Derek Pearsall (1992) offers not a JP and MP for Kent or strategic court player, but someone looking for a quiet life out of London towards the end of his life. Others, in a book called *Who Murdered Chaucer?* (2002), suggest foul play in Chaucer's death on account of his loyalty to Richard II and his criticism of the Church. As further evidence, they cite Chaucer's lack of a will and the fact he took a 53-year lease on his Westminster house in December 1399, only to die nine months later.

So what exactly do we know about Chaucer? He was born some time during the 1340s, probably in London, and died in 1400. He seems to have been an only child (some say he had a sister) of a well-connected mother and successful wine-merchant father who owned several properties, doubtlessly inherited during the Black Death. Seeking to better their son, this socially ambitious family capitalized on their loose connections with the court and placed Chaucer as a page in the household of the Countess of Ulster, wife of Prince Lionel. By 1368, Chaucer was established in the royal household. He accompanied Prince Lionel on his military campaign against the French, where he was captured and later ransomed (1359–60). He saw service with Edward III, Edward's son, the powerful John of Gaunt, and with Edward's young grandson, Richard II. During these years he seems to have acted as ambassador on royal assignments abroad (some of them secret), engaged on court business, according to the archives, in 1360, 1367, 1372–73, 1376–78 and 1385–88. Chaucer also held a series of civil-servant type roles, some of them lucrative (though that didn't prevent him being summonsed several times for non-payment of fines): Controller of Customs (1374), Controller of Petty Customs (1382), Clerk of the Works

(1389) and Deputy Forester (1391). Chaucer's royal connections were enhanced too by marriage and friendship; Sir William Beauchamp acted as a witness in the Cecily de Chaumpaigne affair (more later), for example, and at one time Chaucer stood as surety for both Beauchamp and John de Romsey. He married Philippa de Roet, daughter of the king of Arms for Aquitaine and in service to Edward III's queen. Philippa was also the sister of Kathryn Swynford, mistress of John of Gaunt and later his wife. Chaucer and Philippa had a son, Thomas – about whom we know a great deal – and another one, Lewis, mentioned only in passing in a dedication attached to Chaucer's *A Treatise on the Astrolabe*.

It seems therefore that Chaucer was a seasoned and politic royal servant. Despite the political upheaval of the time, he received gifts and annuities from more than one king. In 1367, Edward III gave him a life annuity and later added gifts for loyal service (1373) and the lucrative wardship of two Kent heirs (1375). He was also in receipt of annuities from John of Gaunt (1374 onwards), one of the most powerful noblemen of the time, and from the future Richard II, doubled on the day he was crowned. He was able to sidestep potentially damaging situations. In 1381, at the time of the Peasants' Revolt, Chaucer still retained his house at Aldgate, one of the gates through which the rebels entered London. We have no idea where Chaucer was at the time. When Richard II's position became increasingly precarious, and he temporarily lost control of parliament, Chaucer resigned his customs posts and moved out of the city into Kent. By 1388, he had surrendered other civic positions and, in a politically savvy move, resigned the annuities he had received from Richard and his father (there were threats to impose heavy penalties upon Richard's allies). When Richard was deposed by John of Gaunt's son, later Henry IV, Chaucer's connections to the house of Gaunt seem to have overridden his loyalty to Richard; in 1398, Henry renewed Chaucer's grants and added another lifelong one.

Possibly the single, most interesting biographical detail about Chaucer rests in a Latin legal deposition of 1380. There, one Cecily de Chaumpaigne releases Chaucer from a charge of *raptus*. In 1993, Christopher Cannon revealed the existence of a

3

memorandum added to that document three days later. Cecily's simple reference to *de rapto meo* (my rape) is replaced by a long-winded, general release from all kinds of possibilities, including felonies, debts and trespass (see Cannon 1993). It also records that Chaucer pays her the sum of £10 while, elsewhere, the life records show that Chaucer calls in a series of debts around this time, with the possibility that more money exchanged hands than the legal document tells us.

Many scholars have ignored or dismissed this intriguing charge by explaining that the Middle English *raptus* means rape or abduction. Some surmise that Chaucer was involved in Cecily's kidnap on behalf of a friend (abductions were often the means to securing marriage with a wealthy and/or reluctant heiress). But a few point out that on its own the phrase *de rapto meo* usually meant rape as we would understand it, a charge so damaging that, as Cannon suggests, not only did Chaucer's powerful friends ensure it was dropped, it is later explicitly retracted through the memorandum.

Rape was a complex, indeed ambiguous, crime in medieval England, one linked to property rights, social class and social mobility. Chaucer's 'crime' may have been figurative rather than real; certainly, it was never tried or proven. Yet the document continues to exercise his readers. It is an example of the socio-political influences connecting Chaucer to the royal household *and* it complicates attitudes towards women and Chaucer's indicted place within the ideologies of his time. In the light of this whiff of scandal, the question 'is Chaucer a friend to women in his work?' suddenly seems highly pertinent indeed.

CHAUCER'S SOCIAL CONTEXT

In the Middle Ages, as now, London was the cultural hub of England. It was, however, far smaller than the present-day city. Around 100,000 people lived there in 1300, but only half that by the time Chaucer died, largely thanks to the Black Death. It was an enclosed city with its gates locked in early evening and through till the next morning, while hardly any of its residents enjoyed full citizenship rights. After the royal court, London's merchant-aldermen and their elected mayor regulated everything from dress codes to fair prices. This civic group drew mainly from the merchant guilds who increasingly acquired power as London became a cosmopolitan crossroads of intellectual, political and economic exchange. In other towns, guilds and fraternities formed cohesive social groups and competed for status, a rivalry depicted in the mystery cycles of the time, where individual guilds of craftsmen took responsibility for financing and acting out particular plays in the procession.

Many writers refer to the three-estates model of social order. This comprised the clergy, nobles and knights, and, at bottom of the pile, labourers and all those in service. We possibly see this represented in the *General Prologue* through the portraits of the Parson, the Knight and the Plowman respectively. But this is more of an ideal than a reality which, instead, consisted of a division between clergy and laity and the sub-divisions within these strata. The clergy composed secular clergy – ranging from the Pope to parish priests and those in receipt of some kind of stipend or annuity, like the Nun's Priest – and regular clergy, those who had taken vows or who belonged to an order or 'rule', like Chaucer's Monk or Friar. The laity had the king at the top, followed by nobles and peers of the realm, then gentry and esquires, and, finally, the 'commons'. This was the largest class and consisted of free landholders and craftsmen, right down to the bulk of the population who were peasants or 'villeins' attached to feudal-style villages and manors. In other words, economic status and the class you were born into were crucial factors in Chaucer's world.

Perhaps the most powerful social and economic institution was the Catholic Church. There were over 100 churches in London alone, which gives us a compelling reminder of its dominance. Religion pervaded the lives of ordinary people whether they were at work or at play. The medieval year was structured through the Church's liturgical calendar (its official devotions, saints' days and festivals), while canonical hours (calls to prayer, times bells were rung) organized the day. The Church owned more than a third of all land in England on which tithes had to be paid, and everyone had to answer to ecclesiastical courts on matters large and small, from heresy to marriage, birth and death.

Yet the late fourteenth century was also a time of controversy and dissent. The Church was riven by internal power struggles culminating in the Papal Schism of 1378–1417 and subject to much criticism of its practices, many of which were corrupt. An increased emphasis upon what we might term 'Englishness', seen in an emerging sense of nationhood and a rise in the use of the English language, corresponded to an upsurge of lay piety whereby ordinary people sought God without the mediation of the Church. The religious reformer, John Wyclif, whose followers are often called Lollards, stressed the active involvement of everyone in religious affairs and ceremonies, and campaigned for the first bibles written in English so that anyone could understand them. Wyclif's anti-clerical stance prompted the Church to crack down on movements like the Lollards, but it is clear that formal religion underwent massive changes during the late Middle Ages.

So, too, the political and social climate of England was in turmoil. The increased use and importance of the vernacular was a thread in a complex web of emerging ideas about what it meant to be English, for example, and how to negotiate legitimate protest and social revolution. Perhaps the most devastating single event upon the stability of life at this time was, however, the advent of a pandemic known as the Black Death. Between four and six million people lived in England in 1300. Fifty years later, after the first wave of what we now believe to be a virulent hybrid of pneumonic and bubonic plague, a third to half of those people were dead. More recently, scholars have estimated that, in some places at least, up to three-quarters of the population died. Black Death reached England in 1348. Other, less violent, outbreaks occurred in 1361–62, 1369 and 1375. In those later ones, children and adolescents seemed especially susceptible. The disease continued to ravage Europe on sporadic occasions for the next several hundred years but nothing impacted on the population like that first epidemic.

The immediate consequence of plague was a declining demographics and falling birth rate. Labour became scarce and so workers were able to demand better wages and lower rents. Many landowners or land-holding families were wiped out, leaving opportunities for other enterprising people to move in and so step up a class. At the same time, less land was being cultivated while across Europe grain prices fell. Much of the population moved from the countryside and into the towns, which expanded rapidly. Urban occupations included a vigorous manufacturing trade with special demand here and abroad for English textiles, particularly wool. Those still tied to the old-style feudal system began to press for more favourable conditions of employment; some left their manors in search of better ones. In the space of a year, between 1376 and 1377, many living in more than 40 villages in the south and south-east of England claimed they were no longer bound to the service of their lords.

The nobility responded by prosecuting those who reneged on their feudal contracts, called for higher wages or who broke the labour laws hurriedly introduced in 1349, 1351 and 1361 to quell the unruly lower classes and try to peg prices at pre-plague levels. Other legislation similarly sought to control the 'commons' or ordinary people. The sumptuary laws of 1363 tried to make everyone dress according to their proper social class. Landlords fined their workers, or charged them for permission to leave their manors. These migrant workers then faced harsh penalties, accused of begging or vagrancy in an attempt to prevent them leaving their home villages. Laws passed in 1349, 1376 and 1388 refused them charity and demanded letters of permission from their lords to authorize their travels.

As a result, social unrest fomented. In 1381, Wat Tyler's 'mob' marched into London to make Richard II listen to their grievances about such repressive legislation and the high poll tax levied by the king to pay for his military campaigns against the French and the Scottish. The event was known as the Peasants' Revolt. Outside London, rebels seized towns like Norwich and St Albans, destroying manorial records and court rolls and attacking Benedictine abbeys (the Benedictine order was thought to be an especially punitive landlord). The rebellion was crushed, though it did eventually put an end to forced labour services; by 1500, a full 100 years after Chaucer's death, there were no more serfs in England.

The Hundred Years' War with France was an additional source of political upheaval and social dissatisfaction. The war was sparked when Edward III counter-claimed against the French for the duchy of Aquitaine, reputed to belong to his mother. Edward's early campaigns (1340–50) were glorious; even the French king, Jean II, was taken hostage and returned to the English court where he resided for a number of years. But later military manoeuvres were both costly and unsuccessful. Edward alternated wars with France with campaigns against the Scots whose own claims to independence interweaved with France's claim on Aquitaine. In Aquitaine itself, its people, the Gascons, had their own language and culture which was separate from France. Initially, the Gascons preferred English to French rule, but when Richard II devolved the dukedom of the region to John of Gaunt in 1390 (in order to avoid paying homage to the French king), the Gascons resented his heavy-handed rule and so joined the rest of France in resistance.

Chaucer lived under three English kings and managed to receive the patronage of all of them, no mean feat considering the faction-making and political machinations that marked the reign of Richard II. When Richard was deposed in 1399, after a rebellion led by John of Gaunt's son who became Henry IV, Chaucer's own position, as loyal to Richard, was potentially dangerous. But he survived to receive Henry's continued favour. Precisely how Chaucer managed this, and other diplomatic missions as a spy working abroad; what, if any, part he played in the Peasants' Revolt; or to what extent he sympathized with religious reformers (several of his friends were known Lollards), remains unknown. We see next to nothing of direct political or historical references in Chaucer's own writing, though academics continually draw analogies and search for clues. *The Canterbury Tales* does have a restless energy and clash of voices and world-views perhaps more typical of its time than our earlier, false understanding of the late medieval period as a time of social stability and 'darkness' might have led us to believe.

CHAUCER'S LITERARY CONTEXT

It is difficult to find evidence of exactly when Chaucer wrote or published his material. In addition, he tended to leave some work incomplete then return later for revision, so the following suggests a schematic order of composition for his major works, rather than a record of dates:

1368–69	*Book of the Duchess* (elegy for John of Gaunt's first wife).
1372–80	*House of Fame* (incomplete).
1380	*The Parliament of Fowls.*
1385–86	*Boece* (translation of Boethius's *Consolation of Philosophy*). *Troilus and Criseyde.*
1386	*Legend of Good Women* completed.
1388–92	*A Treatise on the Astrolabe.*
1386–1400	On-going work on *The Canterbury Tales.*

What is clear is that Chaucer's literary context was rich and varied. So many stories were recounted in so many ways to intersect both oral and written forms of telling: classical legend, epic and romance, ballads, *fabliaux*, saints' lives, folk tales, sermons, alliterative verse, beast fable, lyric, and, in drama, the mystery cycles and miracle plays. At the same time, legal, scientific and philosophical treatises such as Boethius's *Consolation of Philosophy* (with its call to abandon earthly things and look to heaven and a greater good) exert their influence in fiction. *The Canterbury Tales* testifies to the diversity of this literary world and, as we shall see, redraws the 'rules' of literary engagement. Saint's life distils to the stark bones of the *Second Nun's Tale*; the Prioress gives a disturbing miracle in the story of little Hugh of Lincoln; the *Nun's Priest's Tale* mingles beast fable, epic and dream-lore; an English tradition of alliterative verse narrative is sent up in *Sir Thopas*; the *Man of Law's Tale* is a hybrid of the 'accursed queen' folk cycle and Christian founding narrative; the Wife of Bath's fairy tale becomes a homily on medieval notions of *gentillesse*, just as the Franklin's Breton *lai* speaks, in reality, not of magic but noble and courtly ideals; and Chaucer twists three sermon-style poems – the *Wife's Prologue*, the *Pardoner's* and *Parson's Tales* – into contrasting and oblique shapes.

During the late Middle Ages, work was increasingly written in the vernacular or mother-tongue championed by Chaucer and his contemporaries – William Langland in *Piers Plowman*, the anonymous poet of *Pearl, Patience, Cleanness* and *Sir Gawain and the Green Knight*, and John Gower (*Confessio Amantis*) – and continued by the likes of John Lydgate and Thomas Hoccleve after Chaucer's death. A Continental literary tradition was also hugely influential for a cosmopolitan, well-travelled man like Chaucer, helping to shape his own distinctive style and innovative work. French writers aided this literary development: Guillaume de Machaut, Guillaume de Lorris, Jean de Meun, the chronicler Jean Froissart and the makers of the *dits amoureux* (poems on the pains of love or allegories on Fame or Nature), *fabliaux* (bawdy tales with stock characters), courtly lyrics and romances. The thirteenth-century poem *Roman de la Rose* (later translated by Chaucer, we think), was started by de Lorris around 1235 and completed by de Meun after 1275. It was feted for the way a love allegory was turned into satire to offer ambiguity, contradiction and conflict. Its juxtaposition of attitudes and styles seems to inspire the multiplicity of Chaucer's *Tales* which ranges from secular and sexual reality to Christian morality, intellectual ideals and back. In Italy, the literary legacy of Dante and the work of Petrarch and Boccaccio provide Chaucer with source material and ideas about technique. Continental writers favoured a strong rhythm and a flexible form over the English-style alliterative verse better suited to long, narrative pieces. The Italian use of narrators and story-telling frames (gardens, dreams, first-person voices and so on) also seemed to influence Chaucer.

MEDIEVAL LITERARY CULTURE

Chaucer works within a web of influences, sources and inspirations to produce his own literary hallmarks and to spark a literary tradition of his own (see Chapter 2). He also has to negotiate a complex literary culture in which what we understand today by reading, writing and publishing hold no ground. To read a modern-day book is to be part of a commercial transaction. The books we read are mass produced, often by a small number of publishing houses that dominate the market. Individual copies are the same, each with identical layout. Though the author asserts the uniqueness of his or her own creation, copyright often finally rests with the publisher. Even so, once the author's completed manuscript has been accepted for publication and copy-edited, its end result is final, a definitive version replicated in hundreds or thousands for the consumer market and circulated globally. So, page 77 of my 1988 *Riverside Chaucer* bears exact resemblance to someone else's with the same edition.

Turn back the clock 600 years and the picture is entirely different. Most people had access to a massive range of oral stories readily transmitted throughout and across different cultures, even different languages. Some may have been performed as songs by minstrels and itinerant storytellers. Others were related on a regular basis by the clergy seeking examples of moral tales to enhance their sermons or church teachings. Many performances brought together communities in search of a common enterprise and shared enjoyment. In such a world, the book as we know it did not exist. The achievement of mass literacy had yet to come. The printing press was a brand new invention and processes of authorship entirely different from our own.

Without doubt, the status and definition of an author was far from fixed in medieval times. Many factors impact upon the process of medieval writing. Chaucer, and others like him, was a multi-task author. As well as negotiating the complexities of translation (more later), he was reliant upon memory and technique to rework old, spoken story forms. Oral story-telling is entirely different from written narrative which is always an attempt to offer a stable, definitive text. Oral forms are, by definition, more performative or interactive. They demonstrate an acute awareness of audience and its demands, constantly adapting content or altering pace. Such tales are marked by the need to memorize them and so may be repetitive, rhymed or exceptionally rhetorical. Chaucer works with written texts, some of them in languages other than English, *and* unstable or variable oral stories. His intent is to fix them as written narratives composed in the vernacular, itself fluid and without a central or standard dialect.

These demands are compounded by the need to work through and refer back to source material. Medieval audiences – and many after them – had no regard for originality. Instead, they prized scholarship and memory which was, for them, a sign of both genius and moral worth. Thus Chaucer retells stories he reads in other analogues and sources. In so doing, he must pay close attention to this material *and* acknowledge it in his work by referring back to other writers, and quoting from other works in a process known as *auctoritas*. In this way, a medieval author enhances the standing of his (occasionally her) work and adds weight to its ideas. He/she *authorizes* rather than authors a text.

The advent of the printing press led to a more widespread dissemination of texts. With it came an increased literacy in the late Middle Ages. An author like Chaucer would have to be aware that whatever the composition of his intended audience, advances in publishing technology would always widen its scope. We usually assume that Chaucer's audience was partly courtly. In fact, it was more an educated masculine elite of fellow government administrators working, like himself, for the royal household. Yet the *Tales* seems to address women and other classes and occupations too. As printed rather than exclusively oral text, opportunities for private or solitary reading increase. Readers now have more time to reflect on and respond to what they read, and, thus, to participate ever more fully in the process of authorship. Within this dynamic, what is completely redundant is any understanding of an author-God directly controlling his/her material in order to direct our response. Increasingly, the notion of 'author' slips away. What is emphasized, instead, is collaboration, the context of a literary work and its reader-reception.

How do we see these difficulties at work in Chaucer's poetry? The intersection of oral and print culture is evidenced by frequent references to aural readings: calls for 'who shal telle another tale' (I, 3116), 'telleth ye, sir Monk' (I, 3118) or examples like the Wife of Bath's invocations to 'herkneth', 'thou seist', 'tel me this' and 'A ha! By God, I have my tale ageyn' (III, 585). More obviously, Chaucer's concern with *telling* is witnessed by his special and frequent use of narrators, many of whom also directly comment upon the difficulties of writing in *The Canterbury Tales*. Earlier I suggested that, in contrast to an oral story form, a text is fixed in the process of writing it down. But medieval written texts were far more susceptible than our own to corruption or change, with sub-sequent effect upon both author and authorial control. Tim Machan's essay, 'Texts', describes how 'When the parchment on which Chaucer had written became available to others, whether directly or through the hands of a scribe like Adam, it entered a world that offered none of the legal, production, or cultural processes that stabilize the integrity of modern literary works' (Machan: 2002: 430). A text was produced by hand, as a manu-script, before being passed on to a scribe. Many manuscripts were produced under patronage, though we have no real record of this for Chaucer. Monks produced copies in *scriptoria*, but once com-mercial book selling was under way by around 1476, thanks to the printing press, many scribes and craftsmen worked independently in an increasingly consumer-driven market. Scribes often made, by hand, multiple copies of an author's *exemplar* manuscript. The procedure was an open invitation to error especially since English was non-standard in dialect, spelling and punctuation.

Part of that problematic is the vernacular author's fear that due to the diversity of English and its writings, he may be misunder-stood, or even miswritten, by a scribe deficient in that text's par-ticular dialect of English (*T and C*, V, 1793–8). The anxiety is aggravated by the material production of medieval texts witnessed in Chaucer's poem to his scribe (see *Chaucers Wordes Unto Adam, His Owne Scriveyn*). Chaucer hopes Adam contracts a nasty skin disease as retribution for his hours of labour correcting the 'proofs' of his own poetry. Chaucer's concern centres on copying that is not 'trewe' but 'newe', a scribal error or misinterpretation that the author regards as wrong. Here, authorial intention is over-written by the processes of literary production. We are left with the feeling that however much Chaucer attempts to reinstate it – a lengthy activity that involves laborious scraping and some inevitable damage to the original copy – his activities are futile. If not Adam, then others too may alter the composition to leave only an authorial residue or palimpsest to ghost the 'newe' text. Thus an author's manuscript was often subject to physical corruption, deliberate or otherwise, and regardless of authorial intention.

Once copied, subsequent manuscripts were then distributed to those who commissioned the work, either as single copies, or, later, folio and book editions. These were passed, in turn, to other readers. At each stage the author's text was open to further annotation and commentary. Reading – both literally and as interpretation – and writing are, then, inextricably allied in a process that privileges not the author, or a copyrighted text, but the audience. Printing, and copying, was an elaborate and complex procedure. The newness of technology meant that medieval books were often bespoke, rather than mass produced. Those commissioning texts undoubtedly had high expectations regarding content and could, of course, also make demands in terms of presentation. With power firmly in the hands of readers and consumers of texts, the concept of 'author' continues to diminish. Equally, printing was too new to erase all signs of oral culture that by its nature built in and responded to a dialogue in which audience was key.

The medieval world was also a memorial culture. This is not precisely the same idea as memory. Memory is remembrance, an image or quotation or whatever we keep in mind. Rather, *memoria* (memorial) is a technology that reflects and supports the process of remembering (memory). The entire print lay-out of a medieval manuscript page, including the style and positioning of its letters, is a series of visual clues designed to help us recall the text, a high order skill much valued by medievals as a sign of moral excellence. Illustrations, pointers, drawings of fingers or hands, coloured marks or ligatures, all work alongside written comments to cross-reference a text, and enable its audience to remember it. Above all, they mark up how audiences or consumers, and authors formed a web of reading to help a text 'mean'. Its nearest equivalent is hypertext with its frames, particular layout and receptiveness to alteration and reply. Similarly, illustrations, headings and markers (codices) on medieval texts enable readers to navigate their way around these early forms of the book. This suggests the possibility that books were not necessarily read in linear fashion, start to finish, but in other ways, as fragments perhaps and cross-referenced to map meanings that cut across each other.

A medieval text, then, is effectively always a work in progress rather than a 'finished' standard edition. 'Author' has little authority, despite the insistence upon accurate citation of source material. Instead, its influence is consistently dispersed and the notion of an original, authentic text stretched to breaking point.

DISCUSSION QUESTIONS

1. What do you think of Chaucer's treatment of any of the following issues: authority; religion; writing and reading (interpretation); knowledge; marriage?
2. How productive – or even necessary – is it to read Chaucer's tales in the light of fourteenth-century concerns?

CHAPTER 2

LANGUAGE, STYLE AND FORM

TACKLING THE TEXT

At first sight Middle English appears daunting, but is actually much easier than you think. It helps to buy the best edition you can afford. As well as summaries of the tales, such publications also have a same-page vocabulary list where difficult constructions or exceptional meanings are given. Use this list and the glossary at the back of most books only when in doubt. Your reading of it will probably lack speed, at first, but be patient. Don't learn Middle English like a foreign language but, instead, use the following tips to help you begin. Most words are similar to our own but will have been pronounced in the French style with the stress on later syllables or the final 'e' (like French songs) as in 'fresshe' or 'smale'. If you 'say' it as you read, and modernize it, you will recognize most of the words. For example, 'dore' will be 'door', 'fals' will be 'false' and 'shewe', 'show'.

- Watch out for words derived from French like 'daunce' [dance], 'flour' [flower], 'remembraunce' [remembrance], or 'curteisye' [courtesy].
- Occasionally a word has several meanings (like 'corage' meaning 'courage', but also 'heart' or 'sexual desire'), or else has shifted over time ('daungerous' is not 'dangerous' as you might expect but 'aloof' or 'standoffish'). Some have no modern equivalent ('gentillesse' is stronger than 'gentility'). Use your edition's vocabulary list to help you here.

- There was no consistent spelling system so that the letter 'y', for example, might represent our 'g' [yaf – gave] or i [lif or lyf – life].
- Notice tags and filler words like 'eek' [also], 'whilom' [once], or 'sikerly' [truly]. These are soon picked up, but if you are in doubt, make a short vocabulary list to keep alongside your text.
- All consonants are pronounced, as in our 'gnu', so that 'knight' or 'gnof' become 'k-nicht' and 'g-nof'.
- Re-arranging word order into more familiar form may help. For example, 'To chirche was myn housbonde borne' becomes 'My husband was carried to church'.
- Notice peculiar verb forms like 'maken' [to make] or 'maden' [made], or an extra 'y' at the start to denote the past tense as in 'yboght' [bought].
- You may find a run of negatives ['ne', 'nevere', 'nat', 'noghte'] in the same construction, but the meaning is still negative. The number simply strengthens the effect.

LANGUAGE AND VERSIFICATION

In Chaucer's time, three languages competed for privilege. Latin was the tongue of formal, often legal, documents, accessible mainly to an educated elite. Several hundred years after the Norman Conquest, Anglo-Norman French was still the official language of the court and England. Its high status overshadowed the 'third' language, that of everyday people. At this time, English consisted of many dialects, none of them standard (more on this later), but even the French that dominated Chaucer's lifetime existed in more than a single, stable form. The Anglo-Norman French of the 1066 conquest was probably not really spoken after the 1180s. Instead, like Latin, it was kept for legal and official documents and matters of administrative procedure. Most literary works circulating in England up until Chaucer began writing, and after, were also written in Anglo-Norman. Many Latin authors were read in French translations, too. As a writer and a civil servant, Chaucer would have known this strand of French well. But Chaucer was also adept in 'high' or Continental French with its rules of courtesy and diplomacy used in the royal household, and similar to the French of the Prioress in the *General Prologue* who knows only the rougher French of 'Stratford atte Bowe' (I, 124–6). These strands of French spill over into an emerging English to give us words associated with fashion, warfare, administration and law, as well as forms such as 'gentillesse', or nuances contemporary English misses in words like 'daungerous' or 'corage'. Even Chaucer's Latin was corrupted by French to produce a mixed, 'pidgin' form useful for trade and in the keeping of inventories and accounts, while Chaucer's Custance in the *Man of Law's Tale* communicates in a rough approximation of Latin with the Northumberland people (II, 519–20). At the same time, Chaucer's poetic language seems to have been influenced by the social and cultural circles in which he moved: a court permeated by foreign diplomats and courtiers; the free-flow of trade with France, Italy and the Low Countries; and Chaucer's own ambassadorial trips abroad.

All of this gives us a supple and rich mix of languages from which Chaucer drew freely to create a unique version of English poetry. So, what exactly is innovative about it? Chaucer's own English was a London-based dialect, a hybrid of south and south-east forms, and this is what he emphasizes in his work. So, we see him poke fun at other dialects such as the rough northern speech of the lads in the *Reeve's Tale*, and also older, alliterative forms of English verse in *Sir Thopas*. Chaucer does use another traditional English form, and that is iambic metre (an unstressed syllable followed by a stressed one, as in 'the **drogh***te* of **March** . . .'). He then mingles this with a syllable pattern popular on the Continent – a 10- or 8-syllable line – to produce iambic pentameter, familiar to us from Shakespeare but used first by Chaucer. Chaucer also tends to use end rhyme in the shape of rhyming couplets, and to alter the more common end-stop line to the run-on lines seen in earlier French poetry: 'The Cristene folk that thurgh the street **wente**/In coomen for to wonder upon this thyng,/And hastily they to the provost **sente**' (VII, 614–16). This is how most of *The Canterbury Tales* is written, although there are two prose tales (Melibee's and the Parson's) and some in rhyme-royal (seven-line stanzas, rhyming a b a b b c c), like the *Man of Law's Tale*.

CHOOSING THE VERNACULAR

Chaucer is the first major writer to work exclusively in vernacular English, a choice that is far from disinterested. Like his contemporary the writer John Gower, Chaucer's aim seems to be to enhance the status of English and to disseminate his work to a wider audience. His engagement of the issue of translation and its pertinence to the process of writing is exemplified by his use of narrators to voice his tales. The narrators often seem unsure of their role: are they translating in its most literal sense, or are they creating? By employing these distinctive fictional 'authors', Chaucer enters into an important debate about the vernacular.

To write in English meant negotiating some challenging possibilities. In many respects, English was the language of oppression, the language of choice for those ruled still by the Normans. As such, its use was potentially dangerous, sometimes associated with dissent or unorthodoxy: think of Wyclif's 'alternative' English Bible, for example, which I mentioned earlier. It had few credible literary forebears. So, in part at least, it stood at one remove from the medieval tradition of always having to refer back to texts already written. Also the vernacular consisted of many dialects. Without a single dominant dialect or standard, it remained unstable, subject to alteration and innovation. In contrast, French was more fixed at this time, not least because it was used for technical, political and some legal documents. English was, above all, *spoken*, the colloquial language of every day. High status tends to stabilize language. At the same time, it might stifle its development. But a low-status medieval English imported words from elsewhere, from French in particular. It was an evolving language, largely oral and, hence, fluid, in nature, but increasingly competing for recognition and privilege.

At first glance, it appears that, like other medieval writers, Chaucer works solely to translate into English a text from its French or Italian source. In *The Canterbury Tales*, Chaucer-the-pilgrim apologizes for any offence that might arise from his rendition of the other pilgrims' stories. He says he must 'reherce' or repeat every word, not 'feyne' [make up] things or find new words, else he might tell 'untrewe' (I, 730–6). This fear of inaccuracy implies an understanding of translation as technical accomplishment, a need to render a source text accurately. It is echoed at the start of the *Miller's Tale* when, again, Chaucer-the-pilgrim insists he must 'reherce' everything rather than 'falsen som of my mateere' (I, 3173–5). The difficulty of working from a foreign language is highlighted by the narrator of *Troilus and Criseyde*. In Book II, he notes how translating from Latin into English might make words in the vernacular sound lame or archaic; he remarks how language alters over time, and absolves himself of responsibility for the clumsy phrasing of the source text's author (*T and C*, II, 8–26). In addition, he is concerned that because of the diversity of English and its writings, his own work might be misunderstood (*T and C*, V, 1793–8), an anxiety shared too by Chaucer, as we saw in the previous section.

Most importantly, Chaucer's use of the vernacular has an impact upon a redefinition of medieval authorship. Rather than being an act of literal translation, one language to another, it is, as Roger Ellis describes, 'the *performance* of one text in a new language' (Ellis 2002: 443). In *The Canterbury Tales* Chaucer-the-pilgrim begins to move towards such an understanding when his own tale of *Sir Thopas* is interrupted by the Host. He comments on how each of the synoptic gospels is different, even though Matthew, Mark, Luke and John share the same 'sentence' or meaning. Though *his* words in his next story may not replicate those of other versions, his 'sentence' is not different (VII, 943–62). In *performing* a text, Chaucer alters the language of the source text by putting it into English *and* translates or interprets it to create his own narrative. Thus to translate is also to transform. Translation becomes a tool for self-definition, helping Chaucer to position himself not as a mere copyist but a vernacular author who *reinterprets* stories, and, further, suggesting something of the power of language.

This insistence on meaning is seen in the *Clerk's Tale*. Stripped of her peasant clothes and adorned as a royal bride for Walter, Griselda is scarcely recognizable as her former self; she is said to have been 'translated' or transformed (IV, 385). Here, one source body or text is utterly changed in an act that would have been an entirely familiar analogy to medieval readers aware of descriptions of texts as bodies. In this sense, the text is imagined as a captive woman stripped bare to reveal its hidden form, its allegorical meaning 'translated' for all readers as part of a process of *exegesis* or explanation by which all medieval texts were understood.

Despite his protests – seen in both the *Troilus* (I, 393–9) and the *Legend of Good Women* (G text, 349–52) – Chaucer is, however, more than simply a translator. He describes himself as a 'compiler', one who organizes material and edits it, just as the folio compilers do with his own work later (see *A Treatise on the Astrolabe*, 59–64). But, equally, Chaucer says he is a 'makere', a poet (*T and C*, V, 1787 and *LGW*, G text, 342/545). Part of the problem is that medieval 'auctores' [authors] only composed stable, authoritative texts; hence, they were likely to be dead or to have been writing long ago in an accepted tradition or form. In contrast, Chaucer was writing when there was nothing at all stable about late fourteenth-century works. As we have already seen, the notion of stability is allied to a process of cross-referencing and sourcing of other works and languages. Those writing in English had no real vernacular authority and, so, had to find alternative ways of validating their work.

One possibility was to sign or name a work, to identify it as belonging to a particular writer. In the Ellesmere manuscript of *The Canterbury Tales*, one of the earliest copies of Chaucer's poem (c. 1401), is a picture of the man in an age when it was rare to include one. Later on, in Thomas Hoccleve's *Regement of Princes* (1411–12), we find another which Hoccleve – a writer implicated in staking a claim for an English literary heritage beginning with Chaucer – claims to be a striking likeness. Chaucer also references his own work through the voices of his fictional narrators. The start of the *Man of Law's Tale* records how he writes in English to tell of the classical women of the *Legend of Good Women* (II, 46–76) while the *Retraction* mentions some works by name. In an age when vernacular works were often anonymous, these are striking instances of attempts to resolve the problem of authorization so crucial to a medieval context, and to claim prestige for English poetical works.

A medieval author must negotiate the profoundly intertextual nature of fourteenth-century literary culture in other ways too.

Few written source texts stood alone. Medievals valued the practice of *exegesis*. Here all tales are regarded as allegorical and so in need of elaboration or 'glosynge' (to gloss is to explain or comment). Accompanying the story is an array of annotations and commentaries added to the manuscript by scribes copying it out (scribes were readers as well as copyists) and/or other readers who feel compelled to record their own observations and glosses. Sometimes, these are offered to help with a particular textual detail or word meaning or else to explicate a quotation or proverb. Others highlight certain passages, valued and otherwise, or else respond with moral comments. Machan relates how one scribe cuts short the *Squire's Tale* with a comment in Latin that translates as 'This story is really stupid' (Machan 2002: 432). In practice, all attempt to direct the next reader towards a particular interpretation or to influence their judgement. As a consequence, no medieval writer could ignore the readers prior to a text (those glossing his sources) *or* those yet to come, the people who would read his/her work.

STABLE TEXTS AND THE CHAUCER CANON

Chaucer's reputation, and the packaging of his works, alters substantially over the centuries as folio settles to become 'book'. Folios were not transmitted with a view to preserving authorial intention, itself unknown. Instead, judicious selection ensured that *some* of Chaucer's works circulated alongside other anonymous or spurious texts to emphasize particular elements and so construct a 'Chaucer' and 'his works' that is always contingent and variable. Once we understand this then our own modern insistence on a stable text and a definitive edition becomes increasingly problematic. We want to say *this* is Chaucer's poem, *this* is how he conceived and wrote *the* singular and authentic *Tales*. Yet Chaucer's legacy is an incomplete *Canterbury Tales* extant only in pieces and borne of an unstable folio tradition that includes within its bounds an apocryphal canon not excised until the 1800s.

Numerous manuscripts of the *Tales* survive. Some, as we have observed, come to us as fragments of single story or extracts.

Others are fuller, more 'complete' versions. In all, the order of the tales varies. The two most famous and influential editions are the early manuscripts known as Ellesmere and Hengwrt, both produced somewhere around 1400. Most modern critical editions are based upon Ellesmere which follows an order of composition that might or might not have been conceived by Chaucer: remember the influence of scribes, editors and other commentators.

Despite this, most of us have what we assume is an authentic edition of Chaucer's work in *Riverside*. This is a sanitized, modernized, stabilized, even Americanized text. It is, of course, exceptionally useful to modern readers who require a standard edition; critical readings make little sense if everyone uses a different version of the *Tales*. Equally, medieval spelling variants, lack of punctuation conventions and illegible or difficult to read manuscript corrections leave a poem potentially inaccessible. *Riverside* erases these problems and enables a contemporary audience to approach Chaucer with ease. At the same time, in an attempt to avoid potential offence to a modern readership, some language loses the force of its impact in *Riverside*; when Nicholas grabs at Alison's 'queynte' in the *Miller's Tale* (I, 3276), the word is rendered as 'pudendum' to take it completely out of the debate over its equivalent (many believe it corresponds to 'cunt'). In cleaning up manuscript variations and corruptions, it also deflects attention from the material nature of medieval texts as well as the process by which such contamination becomes commonplace, even expected. As such, *Riverside* maybe detracts from a full understanding of how texts make meaning to leave us complicit in its imposition of contemporary notions upon a 600-year-old poem.

More recent scholarship seeks to redress these iniquities. The *Variorum* facsimiles project rejects any claim that theirs is the exact text Chaucer wrote. Instead the *Variorum Chaucer* moves away from a single defining edition by electronically producing several possibilities *simultaneously* and allowing the reader to decide which to use. Similar textual investigations are currently occurring at places like de Montfort, Leicester where scholars are working on a *Canterbury Tales* CD-Rom designed, in part, to replicate the process of medieval manuscript production and its textuality.

Yet even these exceptionally interesting innovations are susceptible to the same difficulties that we always bring to bear on old books. All of these enterprises require an 'original' base text before others can be reconstructed; where *Riverside* uses Ellesmere, the *Variorum* takes Hengwrt as its starting point. The reader must also work through several texts in order to arrive at a decision that will be both informed *and*, as we saw with those early folio compilers, subject to social forces, literary tastes and personal inclination. These editing decisions are no *more* 'medieval' than the *Riverside* editor's standardization of his manuscripts and books, itself reminiscent of medieval scribal practice; remember how scribes would alter spelling, syntax or metre to offer an improved – according to their own standards – version of the author's work. So too every electronic Chaucer text available online in our contemporary world is medieval in spirit, a compilation based on the vested interests of its editors who select the material, write and insert hyperlinks in order to guide us through a text in a particular way and so influence our readings, however multiple they may be.

My point is that all editorial decisions, medieval *and* modern, are bound by similar constraints and the need to negotiate similar difficulties. At the same time as we must accept the need for a standard edition of Chaucer's work we should be aware that it can only ever be a 'best fit', an approximation to an original that in any case has no value or meaning in a medieval context. In the same way, our anxieties about authorial intention and the open, fragmented nature of a medieval text like the *Tales*, whilst understandable, seem increasingly misplaced once we begin to explore the nexus of influences within which medieval authors worked. Derek Pearsall famously argues for a loose-leaf collection of *The Canterbury Tales* into which we might dip at random, read back to front or conventionally, as we wish. In so doing, he highlights how we can never retrieve a definitive Chaucer text or be certain of its final order, or even that we have all its pieces. Any modern edition of the *Tales* is, then, only a *reconstruction*, some more partial than others.

REVIEW

Medieval authorship is a collaborative process in which to write is also to read (interpret). An author must fully engage *all* of the following:

- source stories, some of them oral or maybe in a foreign language
- the process of *auctoritas* in which he/she acknowledges sources and uses them to support his/her own rendition
- the notion of *exegesis*. This is a web of reading and writing practices (hermeneutic) in which the comments and annotations that surround the source text(s) are as crucial as the story itself
- the importance of audience whose responses and interpretations affect not only the reception of the work but the ways in which it is authored in the first place.

GENRE AND NARRATIVE

The problem of authentication is compounded by the genre of the *Tales*. Chaucer's contemporary, John Gower, wrote the *Confessio Amantis* as a collection of tales unified by the use of a single narrator. It has a clear thematic structure that takes the reader step by step through the stories and on to the poem's strong moral message. Boccaccio's *Decameron* is much looser than this but, again, retains a consistent framing device in which a group of travellers move around Italy in an attempt to flee the Black Death. Chaucer's dramatic frame fades in and out. He uses multiple- rather than single-voiced narration, and lacks clarity with regard to didactic intent. But story collections exist in a variety of cultures; all are different in both concept and form. At the same time, many medieval writings offer opposed or conflicting viewpoints as part of a debate in which issues remain, finally, unresolved, more open in nature than we might expect. To judge Chaucer's *Tales* in the light of other well-known medieval collections is a complex business.

The *Tales* also displays an acute awareness of the forces of textual authority. Many narrators begin by discussing source material (either directly, by citing an author or repeating phrases such as 'myn auctour seyde') or else by attempting to suppress a source or analogue that has a different flavour from the rendition about to come. A good example is the Man of Law's insistence on presenting Custance as pure and holy. He tries to ignore the 'known' story of how she comes to be in exile, because of the incestuous advances of her father, but then inadvertently draws attention to it by claiming he will never speak of wicked Canace and her like (Canace was also a victim of incest) (II, 77–89). Other tales equally confront the issue of *auctoritas* by exploring how certain sections of society set up a dominant discourse that they support by citing known, authoritative authors. The Pardoner and the Summoner abuse their religious office even as they support its authority through constant reference to scriptural or doctrinal teachings. January, at the start of the *Merchant's Tale*, opens up a debate about the sexual and gendered behaviours of men and women in a similar way. The issue of how medieval textual authority is used to marginalize women and stifle an alternative, feminine voice is famously taken up in the *Wife of Bath's Prologue*; it also surfaces in the confrontation between Pluto and Proserpina in the *Merchant's Tale*.

We see Chaucer's constant intervention in the field of translation-as-creation, with him reworking tales to defy generic conventions or twisting details, even endings, to work against the grain of an audience's expectations. Above all, his work is consciously marked by a real and pertinent sense of an increasing loss of authorial control. *The Canterbury Tales* comes to us, like the *House of Fame*, incomplete. It is in fragments and with neither a definitive edition nor a clear authorial intent. The narrator of *Troilus and Criseyde* struggles against the authority of source material that determines the outcome of the story in which, completely against his own personal inclination, Criseyde can only be condemned. Chaucer returns to that same difficulty in *The Legend of Good Women*. Here, the narrator-poet is commissioned to speak in praise of virtuous women, a charge that renders his classical heroines increasingly anodyne as he attempts to suppress the violent retribution of those like Medea or Procne and Philomela. And in the *House of Fame* Chaucer explores the fragility of an author's reputation in a medieval hermeneutics that elides his/her status. At the end of *Troilus and Criseyde*, his fictional narrator kisses the footsteps of those 'authorities' that came before him: Virgil, Ovid, Homer, Lucan, Statius. At the same time he relinquishes control of his own 'litel' book, leaving it subject to the vagaries of a public reception that might or might not allow him to stand with the great authors he so admires (*T and C*, V, 1786–92).

PLAYING WITH GENRE

The Canterbury Tales offers a variety of narratives – saint's life, folk tales, romances, epics, fables, dream or love visions, sermons, *fabliaux* or carnival. Some are serious, others bawdy or comic. From where do these stories come? As indicated in Chapter 1, rewriting and retelling stories was considered entirely normal. Authors participated in a process of 'auctoritee' by taking a previous version or versions and reworking that source. In this way, writing became a web of influences and cross-references, intensified by the fact that not all of Chaucer's inspiration sprang from fiction. History, philosophy, religious works and treatises, the law and science all influenced his work. We have, for example, the Parson's sermon, the reasoned debate of Melibee and the alchemy of the *Canon Yeoman's Tale*. The narrator of the *Tales*, Chaucer-the-pilgrim, highlights this when he confronts the nature of his own narrative. As we already know, he begins by declaring himself a faithful translator of the words and ideas of others. And behind him, Chaucer-the-author presents us with a multitude of stories gathered up into a collection only loosely held together by the fictional voices of the Canterbury pilgrims.

Recognizing form is easy, but establishing genre is more difficult. Why does Chaucer employ so many different types of story in *The Canterbury Tales*? Most collections of his time had a central theme holding together a diversity of tales. Or, else, all tales in the collection were bound by a single genre, such as epic, romance or courtly love poems. Others grouped stories within a specific framework as in a dream vision or other dramatic devices. The *Tales* does not directly conform to any of these generic codes. Unfinished, it is partially held within an incomplete frame, that of the story-telling contest itself. It is possible to identify certain themes within the collection – love and marriage, knowledge and authority, social commentary – but no one idea unites it. Instead, Chaucer offers a diversity of themes, ideas and dramas in a dazzling and varied array of tales. And, just as he fractures audience expectations by shifting and distorting a chosen tale's analogues, so, too, he sometimes subtly alters anticipated generic patterns, something we will return to later.

Several of Chaucer's other tales are *fabliaux*, a form exemplified early on with the tales of the Miller and the Reeve. A cursory glance at the plots of each soon reveals the format. In the first, an old man marries a young woman who cuckolds him with a young lover. Both the husband and another rival are deceived by an elaborate plan designed to make fools of them. In the second, a miller jealously guards the virtue of his daughter. He apparently outwits a pair of students sent to prevent his notorious thieving of the corn he grinds. They in turn trick him, one taking the maidenhead of his daughter and the other having sex with his wife. Indecency saturates the *fabliau* form. Terminology is colloquial, prosaic and often lewd or obscene. Scatalogical detail is important. In the *Miller's Tale*, Absolon is mocked for his dislike of 'fartyng' (I, 338), a factor exploited when he begs a kiss from his beloved Alison. He kisses her 'naked ers/Ful savourly' before he is fully aware of what he is doing (I, 3734–5). Later, he is duped into kissing Nicholas who puts out his 'ers' in readiness and 'leet fle a fart' louder than a thunder clap (3806–8). Alan and John, the two protagonists of the *Reeve's Tale*, are students from the north, a dialect that Chaucer uses to comic effect in the story. The details of the plot quickly accumulate. While Alan 'had swonken [been on the job]' all night long with the miller's daughter (I, 4235), his friend concocts a plan to ensure that when his wife gets up to 'pisse' (I, 4215) she would end up in his bed. There 'on this goode wyf he leith on soore./So myrie a fit ne hadde she nat ful yoore [she hadn't had such a good time for ages]' (I, 4229–30). There are, then, no surprises in these stories.

Other poems demonstrate a mingling of sources with subsequent effect on what we think we are reading. The story of Custance's trials in the *Man of Law's Tale* was well known in folklore. It conforms to a pattern of motifs found in folk, fairy and romance tales where the heroine is expelled from the parental home and must await rescue and reconciliation with her family. In the meantime she suffers a series of tribulations and tests upon her virtue. Custance is sent to marry the Sultan of Syria, escaping with her life on her wedding night. She survives two exiles at sea, a false accusation of murder, and attempted rape before a final reunion and safe reconciliation with her husband and her father.

Folklore is, however, not the only element of her tale. Equally Chaucer's audience would have recognized not only the pattern of her story – itself a part of his chosen genre (romance) – but other versions of it. Some analogues of this tale have an alternative motivation for her initial journey to Syria. Chaucer and his contemporary Gower, who includes the poem in his *Confessio Amantis*, have marriage as its impetus. Yet another work of the same period, Thomas le Chestre's *Emaré*, adopts the more usual telling of her story to record how she is cast adrift in a rudderless boat after refusing her father's incestuous advances. Though each might be categorized as romance, each too offers a different emphasis and interpretation of events. An immediate question is raised when Chaucer not only omits the 'typical' incest element of Custance's tale: but then permits his fictional narrator implicitly to draw attention to it. The Man of Law declares he will speak only of good women and not of those like the wicked, incestuous Canace (II, 77–89). Here, Chaucer plays upon the audience's anticipation of events. It already knows how a particular genre (in this case romance) operates. If, in addition, it is aware of alternatives to the same story, then a complex set of expectations inform the tale's reception.

To interpret the *Man of Law's Tale* as romance, however, is only half the story. Another analogue is Nicholas Trivet's *Anglo-Norman Chronicle*, a form of history as its title suggests. Here Custance is a historical figure alongside her father and her son Mauricius. In part, Chaucer's story is not entirely fictional. Trivet's account points to Custance – or Constance – as a central figure in the Christianization of Europe. Her father is Emperor of Rome, centre of the Catholic faith. He effects a marriage with the Muslim Sultan of Syria, who converts rather than lose her. The trouble begins when he insists that the rest of his kingdom follow suit (218–40). Custance is accompanied on her journey by a multitude of bishops and advisers (253). Later, she manages to convert others to the faith, a detail highlighting the religious thread complicating Chaucer's poem.

Thus another genre contaminates what was originally a folk or romance tale so that several sets of expectations work together on this hybrid form. Chaucer mingles romance, history, religion and to it adds the voice of a fictional narrator with his own agenda. This is then placed within another fiction, that of the wider dramatic frame. The story also becomes part of a story-collection, a genre with its own demands, limits and patterning. In this way, the tale exemplifies how stories operate at a variety of levels. The *Man of Law's Tale* can be read separately from the dramatic frame or disconnected from the story-collection genre. The narrator's influence may work with or against the drift of the story itself. Expectations clash leading to a variety of readings. Is this a folk tale with a focus upon psychological drama and self-identity? Is it romance masquerading as social commentary upon the role of the family and the place of daughters within it? Is it history or else a religious story? What effect does the knowledge of its analogues have upon interpretation? Does singling out one of these possibilities detract from other important strands of the work? Chaucer manipulates generic conventions and plays upon what an audience expects from differing types of stories. In the same way, he takes several sources and reworks them to produce something new. This fracturing of rules and codes opens up entirely the notion of form and multiplies possibilities to challenge the nature of writing.

DISCUSSION QUESTIONS

1. How far ought we to think about correspondences beyond the usual ordering of the fragments (groupings) of *The Canterbury Tales*?

2. Do you agree that Chaucer goes beyond what we expect when we think about story-telling in the *Tales*?
3. Do you think we can distinguish with any certainty between *sentence* and *solaas* in the *Tales*?

CHAPTER 3

READING *THE CANTERBURY TALES*

NARRATIVE VOICE AND HOW IT WORKS

The *General Prologue* introduces us to a range of characters all gathered at the Tabard Inn in Southwark in preparation for a pilgrimage to Canterbury. We meet a variety of figures, each identified by occupation and/or social rank. Their physical appearance is carefully detailed, along with their clothes or the things they own and an accurate record of their speech. These clues indicate something of the ways in which we might read them and so begin to make meaning of the poem as a whole. The Wife of Bath, for instance, wears scarlet stockings and elaborate head-gear to indicate ostentation and wealth. She has gap-teeth (I, 603), a sure sign of lechery in medieval physiognomy, an impression corroborated by the birthmarks mentioned later in her *Prologue*, a 'Venus seel' (III, 604), plus another 'Martes mark', one on her face and one in a more intimate place (619–20). Similarly, the infected pustules of the Summoner's terrifying face signify his degenerate morals (I, 623–33). Such passing details, typical of medieval characterization, give us a series of 'types'. But Chaucer goes further by including Chaucer-the-pilgrim's sly or ambiguous asides – like his reference to the inscription on the Prioress's brooch, *Love Conquers All* (I, 162) – and juxtaposing or scrambling comments.

A good example of how this technique operates is the description of Alison in the *Miller's Tale*. Alison is composed of natural images with a mouth as sweet as mead or apples. She is compared to a primrose and a 'newe pere-jonette tree', as well as a series of animals: a colt or kid skipping after its mother, her body as slender as a weasel and soft as ram's wool, and her voice like a swallow (I, 3247–8). Such images seem admiring, but the cumulative effect of comparison to so many animals might be to intimate that she is actually base or lustful, and certainly her later behaviour with Nicholas adds to this. Or is she simply young and innocent? Alison's clothes also match her loveliness, but they in turn call attention to a certain vanity. Her skirts flare over 'hir lendes' [loins] (3237), and her shoes lace high up her legs (3267). We notice her 'likerous' or flirtatious eye (3244). Similarly, her naturalness is undercut by hints of artifice: a purse adorned with 'latoun', a brassy metal (3251), and her plucked eyebrows (3245), or her brooch broad as a 'bokeler', the raised centre of a shield (3266). We are told that she is brighter than a newly minted 'noble' (3255–6). In this loosely structured extract, then, a string of images fight for definition, a process enhanced by the careful placing of the concluding remarks. There, she is described as lower class, a 'wenche' (3254) or a gay 'popelote' [dolly], fit for any *lord* to have in his *bed* or any *yeoman* to *wed* (3269–70, emphasis mine). What at first sight appears to be an approving portrait is rendered less secure by scattering images that simultaneously hint at its opposite. This technique is repeated elsewhere with, for example, the cumulative effect of 'fresshe' May in the *Merchant's Tale*, a word whose meaning shifts as the plot is revealed.

But from where – or whom – do these first impressions of those who tell a story in the *Tales* come? You may have noticed in the *General Prologue* a speaker identified only as 'I', a member of the company of pilgrims who, before the day is out, has spoken to all of them (I, 20–34). This anonymous character informs us of his plan to tell us all about his fellow travellers (38) and is the same voice whose asides offer hints to the reader about their hidden depths. In this manner he guides us towards a considered reflection of those involved in the drama of *The Canterbury Tales* to establish an important background. He records the precise details of the assembled pilgrims (716) and promises to tell everything about their journey (724).

That same voice also sets up another feature of the poem, its dramatic framing device, by introducing the Host, Harry Bailly. Harry sets up a story-telling competition whereby each pilgrim is required to relate two tales, one on the way and one on the return journey. The winner will receive a free supper. The proceedings are overseen by Harry who arranges for the drawing of straws to choose who begins (790–845). Harry also defines the rules for judgement by calling for stories 'of best sentence [morality] and moost solaas [entertainment]' (798). So, the stage is set with three layers of narration and three separate sets of speakers.

As the instigator of the tale-telling competition that takes place in this dramatic frame, Harry Bailly's role is to orchestrate events. He takes charge with all agreeing that he should judge the competition (817–18). He efficiently moves on the proceedings (I, 4345–53/II, 25–31) underscoring the importance of making haste, and his own coordinating role with his request at the end to the Parson to 'knytte up wel a greet mateere' (X, 28). A further aspect of Harry's role is his intervention in the quarrels that take place between the other pilgrims. The Friar–Summoner argument threatens to prevent the Wife of Bath from telling her story. Harry cries 'Pees!' and again, later, as the Friar's own tale falters (III, 850/1298), and rebuking the Friar for his rude interference (1286–9).

As well as highlighting Harry's diplomacy and active part in the contest, this interlude also introduces another important notion, that of 'quiting'. To 'quite' means both to 'match' and to 'avenge'. The animosity between the Friar and the Summoner is based on an intense personal and professional dislike. When the Friar laughs at the conclusion of the Wife of Bath's long-winded *Prologue*, the Summoner accuses the Friar of suffering from the same wordiness. The Friar retorts that his story will make us all laugh at summoners, about whom he can reveal much, and the exchange degenerates (829–49), resuming after the *Wife of Bath's Tale* with the Friar attacking the Summoner as good for nothing except the dispensation of summonses for fornication. The Summoner declares he will 'quite' him at every turn, to expose him as a sham (1280–4/1290–7).

At one level, personal rivalry and friction add depth to the dramatic frame (see the Miller and the Reeve for a further instance). Yet an argument such as this one, based on what the other represents, also opens up the possibility of debate about crucial issues: here, about the Church and its practices. Equally, at a dramatic level one character tells a tale designed to expose another, to gain personal revenge, to ridicule or 'quite' that person (or tale).

Harry's interventionist policy does more than reveal the complex workings of the fictional dramatic frame, though. Sometimes his interruptions suggest something about his own character's failings. The observant 'I' of the *General Prologue* describes Harry as merry and bold in speech (I, 755–7). His speech is certainly direct and liberally peppered with oaths like 'For Goddes bones!' and 'by Goddes dignitee!'(II, 1166/1169). The Host's oaths are declarative and summarize his clear, colourful views. His prosaic and vulgar interruption to *The Tale of Sir Thopas*, the first tale told by the 'I' of the overall poem, humorously judges and dismisses it as 'nat worth a toord!' (VII, 906/923/950). Elsewhere, his coarse and emphatic rejection of the Pardoner's invitation to offer to his relics demonstrates how Harry slips out of his role as Host and organizer of the contest and firmly into the frame itself. His part in this quarrel reminds us of his dual role, both overseer and participant in the frame.

On the one hand, the Host's oaths help to establish him as master of the proceedings. His emphatic words seem to ensure that his comments are final or authoritative. On the other, Harry's swearing indicates a loss of self-control. Similarly, his control of the contest is less secure than he imagines as individual speakers contradict his requests. Harry calls on the Clerk, for example, to tell them a merry tale, not a sermon or anything dull in 'high' rhetorical style, but something plain and easy to follow (IV, 9–20). Yet the Clerk's offering is serious, a tale related in elevated, elegant diction. After his comic rejection of *Sir Thopas*, Harry insists on a moral prose story (933–5). He receives his wish, but in the form of the wordy *Tale of Melibee*. Equally, he calls for a 'fable' from the Parson who immediately announces his intention to present a serious sermon instead (X, 29).

At times, the Host's control of events is undercut by the actions of others. Though judge and chair of the contest, he has no real authority over the words spoken by the pilgrims. He exemplifies an authority that is simultaneously undercut, as evidenced by his personal 'failing' and a judgement of the tales that is all too often coloured by his beliefs and prejudices. For instance, Harry's comments upon his own wife, whom he mentions on more than one occasion, hint at a concealed fear of women. He dismisses two of the richest tales in the collection, the *Man of Law's Tale* and the *Clerk's Tale*. The first is praised as something worth while for the occasion (II, 1165), and the second as 'a gentil [nice] tale' (IV, 1212c). Harry wishes his wife had heard the *Clerk's Tale* of extreme and impossible perfection in a woman (VI, 1212c–e). The Merchant's bitterly comic tale of an adulterous young wife, offered in revenge for his own marital discord, strikes a particular chord. Harry's (partial) understanding of that tale is intimated in the diatribe against deceitful, untrustworthy women that follows. In fact, as far as Harry is concerned, the *Merchant's Tale* is authoritative proof of women's treachery (IV, 2419–26). Briefly, he alludes to a fear of his own wife whose vices he could never fully detail, before abruptly breaking off (2426–40). Harry therefore symbolizes all that is masculine and authoritative. Yet Chaucer undermines our faith in this representation for Harry is not all that he appears, either in his personal life or as the controlling element of the dramatic frame.

When all agree that Harry can be both judge and reporter of their tales, as they put it (I, 813), he is invested with authority. The question is, as we have seen, is he up to the job? Many of the Host's readings of what he hears are affected by his perception of himself and others. He particularly enjoys the *Nun's Priest's Tale*, a multi-layered narrative that Harry interprets at its simplest and most literal level as a tale about the 'marriage' of a potent cockerel whose virility he transposes onto the figure of its teller, the Nun's Priest. Here the art of narration is conflated with masculinity so that story-telling 'becomes' a masculine pursuit. A well-controlled narrative is a well-told tale, which is what we all admire. At the same time, a medieval understanding of the ways in which we *read* complicates this issue. The 'proper' way to read was through a process known as *exegesis*. Here, readers search for deep, allegorical meaning – the hidden 'fruit' of a text – just as clerics 'glose' or interpret the Bible for those unable to grasp its full import. This is an authoritative, masculine pursuit. Harry's reading of this – and other stories – *seems* masculine and authoritative for he usually gives us a single and definitive interpretation. On the other hand, an 'improper' (and feminine) medieval reading was to interpret stories in a literal or surface manner. Harry comments authoritatively on the *Nun's Priest's Tale*, only to read it solely as the simple animal fable it is, and ignore other important possibilities. Thus the Host offers dual readings, a closed and 'masculine' viewpoint alongside a literal, 'feminine' interpretation. In this way, Harry's humorous role as interpreter of stories is more serious for it undercuts the masculine authority with which his role as judge is automatically invested.

CHAUCER-THE-PILGRIM

Harry's voice can never be authoritative for his comments are filtered through another key speaker, the 'I' who recounts the pilgrimage and the story-telling competition itself. Like Harry, this 'I' is also a participant in the dramatic frame, another pilgrim on the way to Canterbury. He seems a self-effacing figure, several times apologizing for the nature and wording of some of the material he recounts. He begs listeners to excuse his plain speaking and is anxious to avoid offence (725/743). So, he warns against tales told by those such as the Miller (3167–85), even inviting us to read something else (3181). He wishes us to understand that his role is simply that of a reporter who repeats, word for word, what he hears.

One of the effects of a first-person narration is to offer an eye-witness account. This character is part of the pilgrimage and, hence, able to record directly what he sees and hears (I, 31–2). Yet he is also an observer, slightly apart from his fellows, whose direct intervention is rare. In contrast to the Host, we scarcely notice his presence. The 'I' offers an apparently straightforward chronicle noting how the Pardoner and Harry kiss and make up after their quarrel, for example (VI, 968). All that we learn of the tales themselves and their speakers through the device of the dramatic frame – even what we know of Harry Bailly – is filtered through the voice of the first-person narrator. But who is this speaker? Is his role that of recorder or reporter, as he would have us believe, or something more complex?

The anonymous speaker is eventually identified as 'Chaucer' in links such as 'Bihold the merry words of the Hoost to Chaucer' and 'Here begins Chaucers *Tale of Thopas*' or 'Chaucers *Tale of Melibee*'. Our earlier impression of his humility is confirmed in the exchange he has with Harry Bailly. The Host asks 'what man artow?' (VII, 695) articulating the question on all our lips. Harry notes the man's shyness, commenting on how his eyes are always cast on the ground as if searching for a hare. He demands he step forward, inviting the others to make way for him (698–9). Harry says that he seems 'elvyssh' [in a dream] (703), and unsociable, an enigmatic figure indeed. When the Host calls for a tale of mirth from him, this 'Chaucer' begs him not to be angry or displeased, for he only knows one tale (706–8). Interrupted in mid-story, he is distressed, seeming not to know why he cannot continue as the others have; after all, 'it is the best rym I kan?' (928). Yet, not only do the tales he recounts demand closer inspection (read them for yourself and see), but the exchanges that frame them hint at something deeper. When the 'Chaucer' of the *Tales* hopes that we will like his rhyme, the only one he knows and the best he can do, he is asking us to listen to *Sir Thopas*. We have already noted Harry's dismissal of it as 'drasty' rhyme 'dogerel', one that is plodding and dull (923/925/950). This is possibly the worst tale in the collection *if* we are to (mis)read it as a serious offering (as Harry does).

Suddenly this speaker's self-effacing attitude, his acute lack of awareness about the reception of his first tale (his second is the *Melibee*), seems disingenuous. Is this actually Chaucer, the poet? Or, is the author of the *Tales* having a sly joke at our expense, poking fun at both himself – the great writer – and our expectations of writing and writers? The 'I' is not Chaucer but the author at one remove, hidden behind a mask or *persona*, speaking through the voice of one named as 'Chaucer' but more usually distinguished by us as Chaucer-the-pilgrim. In this way, the voice that filters all the other voices and stories is itself manipulated and controlled by a hidden author. In effect, we can identify two Chaucers. One is firmly located in the text as a narrative voice in its own right: Chaucer-the-pilgrim, or the 'I'. The other is the author, the concealed controller who writes everything in the *Tales*. Chaucer-the-pilgrim is fictive, an invention of Chaucer-the-author. When he speaks as 'I', it is tempting to assume that his views are attributable to Chaucer himself (just as it is with all the other speakers). Of course, this is not necessarily the case but the problem is how to tell the difference, an issue compounded in the conclusion to the *Tales*, the *Retraction*.

Who exactly is the speaker here? The voice is first person, but is it Chaucer-the-pilgrim? Humility and apology mark the writing (X, 1075–6). The tone is serious with none of the humour of the exchanges with the Host or the comic parody of *Sir Thopas*. Gone too is the straightforward, observant chronicling of events. This is a moral retraction which revokes all 'translacions and enditynges of worldly vanitees', and begs forgiveness for certain works, such as 'many a lecherous lay' (1083/1078), as well as commendation for more 'Christian' pieces (1079–90). We might ask several questions at this point. To what extent is this section part of the *Tales*? Is it an afterthought, written by the author towards the end of his career in the voice of someone attempting to put his affairs in order? It is a highly moral conclusion; are we, then, to read the rich tapestry of tales that come before it in the light of this desire for grace, to dismiss the humorous, the vulgar, or the ambiguous asides? The main focus of our attention here is who speaks. It ends 'compiled by Geffrey Chaucer' for 'Heere taketh the makere of this book his leve'. What remains unclear is whether this is the author, or whether we are still in the dramatic frame of the *Tales* and this is Chaucer-the-pilgrim.

Another problem raised by first-person narration is that of reliability: to what extent may a voice be trusted? I indicated earlier that Harry Bailly's judgement of tales is often prejudiced. But Chaucer-the-pilgrim faithfully records events. From the start he insists upon the importance of accuracy. Whoever does his job, he says, must report as closely as he can every single word spoken. Otherwise, he would be narrating 'untrewe', inventing things or using 'newe' [his own] words (I, 731–6). Rather, 'wordes moote be cosyn to the dede' (742). So, though it displeases him to retell the Miller's churl's tale, he must detail every word, however coarse or offensive, or else be guilty of falsifying some of his material (3170–5).

His role is thus to chronicle or translate. The predominant feature of the poem centres on this notion of recording, so that 'quod' becomes a key word. Chaucer-the-pilgrim quotes an exchange or an argument within the frame and leaves us to interpret its significance. One such example is the interlude between the Squire and the Franklin, rudely interrupted by the Host, whose remarks only gain their full irony in the light of the entire exchange (V, 671–708). There, the Franklin wishes his own disowned son was half as noble as the squire before the Host interrupts with a scathing dismissal of a 'gentillesse' he fails to understand. To translate or record is also to claim objectivity; in short, contrary to what a first-person account might suggest, Chaucer-the-pilgrim denies any vested interest in what he tells. In this way Chaucer is able to use this figure as a means of ordering the dramatic frame, to highlight its interplay.

Similarly, by allowing this voice to record several interpretations or meanings of tales (such as Harry's, for example), the intertextuality of the whole is widened. So, though we are set up for the vulgarity of the *Miller's Tale* which Chaucer-the-pilgrim must objectively report, he also guides us towards interpretation of it by advising us not to take it too seriously (I, 3181). Our enjoyment of the Miller–Reeve quarrel, and the reception of the tales each tells, is then heightened. We are also invited to consider more than one meaning of these stories. Interpreting the *Miller's Tale* as a personal attack, the Reeve 'quites' him with his own story. Yet, Chaucer-the-pilgrim tells us that the others simply laugh at it (3855–8). No one, except the Reeve, notices any intended slight. Equally, Chaucer-the-pilgrim records that the Cook particularly enjoys the *Reeve's Tale* because he knows a thieving miller (4325–38). The Cook's reading is only one narrow reading, informed by his own personal animosity towards millers in general. Ironically, it also happens to concur with the Reeve's intention which no one else seems to have noticed. Thus alternative readings present themselves, none of which is the sole sum of the tale. Just as the Host's comments point towards a single reading of a tale, Chaucer-the-pilgrim's 'record' offers alternative, though similarly narrowed, possibilities. In this way, Chaucer offsets voices and opens up interpretation. It is this fracturing of the authority of tales – of finally 'understanding' them in a unified reading – that the *Tales* invites us to consider.

MULTIPLE VOICES: OTHER NARRATORS

The third level of narration is centred on the multiple voices of those telling their tales. These we hear as individual speakers, such as the Knight, the Miller, or the Reeve. A different first-person speaker, the strength of whose presence varies from poem to poem, recounts a story. Differing speakers struggle to shape and control their stories, to participate in the dramatic frame under the imperfect control of Harry Bailly. Each direct intervention in their own narrative is a significant and, sometimes, ambiguous moment. So, when the Clerk tells us of Griselda that 'O nedelees was she tempted in assay!' (IV, 621), he criticizes Walter's behaviour. Or when the Man of Law repeatedly directs our attention towards biblical miracles, he denies agency to a Custance who 'dryveth forth' her own way (II, 505/875). Each voice is filtered through the so-called accurate 'translation' of Chaucer-the-pilgrim, a comic mask that conceals the author who, of course, manipulates everything to leave us without a definitive version or reading of a tale, let alone of the *Tales* as a whole.

Despite this, essay questions and some critical readings still invite us to focus on the way a speaker narrates a tale, even as the question of matching a tale with its teller misleads us. The tales are not necessarily dramatic monologues as early critics suggested. Though some speakers seem to be well placed to recount the stories they tell, many do not. The Parson offers a serious,

didactic sermon. The Miller and the Reeve engage in a quarrel-
some dialogue within the dramatic frame which is reflected in
their poems. At the same time, the coarse Miller gives us the
bawdy tale we might expect, one that also demands to be read in
conjunction with its apparent obverse, the Knight's. Equally,
many fruitful correspondences work outside the drama of story-
within-a-story. The opening lines of the *Prologue* stress natural,
youthful vigour and a sexual energy intimated in the spring
showers that 'perced' March to the root and 'engendred' fresh
growth (I, 1–12); all of this comes to nothing in the spiritual
aridity of the *Retraction* and the Parson's denial of sexual joy at
the 'end' of the *Tales*. At the same time, the lusty youngsters of
the *fabliaux* are offset by the 'queer' figures of romance (more
later) and the sexual, ultimately barren, urges of the elderly: the
Wife with the same 'coltes toothe' (III, 602) as the Reeve (I, 3888)
who, like January in the *Merchant's Tale*, is driven by a 'green
tayl' (see I, 3869–70/3877–8 and the reference to sap rising in an
old tree, IV, 1461–6) that denies the 'hoor' [frost/grey] of his
head.

In short, the dramatic frame is partial and incomplete just as
the *Tales* itself is a work in progress. Some stories work both with
and against the voice of their tellers to suggest an interest not in
drama but in *story*, in the ways in which a first-person narrative
voice might influence a tale and set up cross currents of ideas
beneath its surface telling. A character study of speaker alone is
a redundant exercise and the possibility of exploring a fictional
narrator's 'personality' to see if it matches the tale told fraught
with problems, not least because Chaucer re-allocated some of
his material. The introduction of the *Man of Law's Tale* suggests
that he intends to speak in prose, a claim not borne out in his narrative. Many believe that Chaucer originally intended the Man
of Law to deliver the *Tale of Melibee*. Others argue that the
Shipman's Tale was intended for the Wife of Bath. Its equation
of sex and money apparently corresponds to Alison's depiction
of loveless marriage, tricky women and her comment that 'al is
for to selle' (III, 414). The Shipman is named as the final speaker
of the preceding fragment and promises 'My joly body schal a
tale telle' that will wake up the entire company (II, 1185–7). Yet

it is the Wife who opens the next fragment with her shocking *Prologue*. Some speakers do not appear in the *General Prologue* so the question of 'fit' is clearly dubious. The Second Nun and the Canon's Yeoman are all additions to the *Tales*, while the Nun's Priest merits a mere two-line description. Others – the Yeoman, the Plowman, the Sergeant at Law – are described but take no part in the contest. The fit between story and speaker is a hit and miss affair. Though some match, others are more problematic. Some tales may even work against the grain so that though the narrator influences the story, it may not be in a manner that is immediately apparent.

SHAPING NARRATIVES: JUXTAPOSITION AND DISTORTION

Manipulation of audience expectation can also occur within a particular generic code itself. One way to achieve this is through the endings of the poems, something I explore later. Another is via the use of language. The prosaic terminology characterizing *fabliaux* is juxtaposed with a surprise element in the *Miller's Tale*. Nicholas is depicted as an accomplished courtly lover with his sweet words and wonderful singing voice (I, 3305–6). He speaks the language we recognize as belonging to courtly love, telling Alison that 'deerne [hidden/secret] love' (3278) drives him. If she cannot requite it, he will die (3280–1). He asks for 'mercy' until she grants him his desire (3288). Absolon, his inept rival for Alison's affections, replicates this elevated vocabulary. Powdered and scented, he stands at Alison's window to tell her of the love-sickness that prevents him from eating (3698–707). For the sake of true love he appeals for her 'grace' and her 'oore' [mercy] (3726). This is offset, however, by an earthiness more typical of the genre. As Nicholas sweet-talks Alison, he pats her 'aboute the lendes [loins] weel' (3304) and clasps her thighs (3279). At the same time, he caught her by the 'queynte' (3276), an obscenity compounded by his puns on 'to die' and 'spille', colloquialisms connoting orgasm (3278/81). A clear physical element exists alongside the distant, formal notion of courtly love. Absolon also introduces a low, corporeal element – albeit accidentally – alongside his love-talk, with his bathetic admission that he feels

faint and sweats, and yearns for her 'as doth a lamb after the tete'
(3703–5). This physicality is further explored towards the end of
the tale with Absolon's misdirected kiss, the naked buttocks
thrust out of the window, the fart and the branding of Nicholas's
'towte'. Clearly this juxtaposition of the physical and the spiritual intensifies the comedy. But is there an additional reason for
its inclusion?

The *Miller's Tale* is preceded by the *Knight's Tale*, an elaborate
story of epic proportions and courtly love. Its high theme is
matched by its serious diction. To follow it up with a low-life
fabliau about ordinary, primarily sexual love offers a perfect contrast in the dramatic frame that loosely binds the *Tales*. But it
does not fully account for the playing with genre just encountered. There, Chaucer allows the abstract and spiritual notion of
courtly love to be contaminated by the physical, by sex and
bodily functions. In this way, he is able to suggest that a potentially outmoded and certainly unrealistic ideal represented in the
Knight's Tale is hopelessly distanced from everyday reality.
Nicholas is the successful lover, blending courtly love language
and physical action. His elegant speech is a charade designed to
achieve his aim of 'deerne' love, a ploy to get Alison into bed.
Thus this genre is stretched to its limits to produce a humorous
tale that encourages us to read the Knight's and the Miller's
together, and, in turn, to reconsider depictions of love, chivalry,
men and women, and so on, as they occur elsewhere in the *Tales*.

For instance, the *Knight's Tale* produces a dialectic all of its
own, whereby two elements – an overt surface narrative and its
concealed, silent twin – must be read together. The narrative
demands many changes of scene and a careful sequencing of
events, a challenge witnessed in the narrator's constant interjec-
tions. He comments how he must leave one episode or character
and turn his attention back to others. This clear negotiation of the
trajectory of his plot seems to suggest he retains a grip on the narrative. He constantly reminds us that he must move the story on if
he is to pack in all its events. Yet, though he insists that he will
relate it briefly (I, 1000), he gives us, for example, a long-winded
account of Theseus's exploits when he ransacks Thebes
(983–1027). He offers precise details of how the Athenians build

the amphitheatre for the lists, claiming it is important to record 'th'effect' [substance] of the elaborate preparation (2206–7), else people might consider him negligent (1881–6). The Knight, then, expends narrative space disproportionately. He exhaustively details battles, elaborate rituals or lavish public spectacles to foreground an epic or monumental activity that shores up a patriarchal culture. He stresses the visual, concrete signs of the world, shaped into a coherent narrative by the honourable code and impulses of chivalry. So, he describes the artistic intricacy of the temples dedicated to Mars, Venus and Diana. Each time, he declares his intention to relate this briefly (2052/1953–4/2039–40 respectively) and then gives it more than passing mention. The Knight recounts the nature of Arcite's accidental death in graphic detail too, followed by an extensive description of his funeral (2206–7).

Readers may well question this seemingly pointless trivia, whereby the Knight ends with a boys-own adventure story that distorts the boundaries of the epic-romance genre. Many critics perceive a correspondence between him and the figure of Theseus in that both participate in a process of patriarchal control. The Knight seeks to impose order by establishing the chivalric ties between men that drive his plot. Here chivalry is a social mechanism that curtails and controls adverse emotions and behaviours. Savage fighting in the grove is regulated by a public joust. Arcite's terrible death is recompensed with a state funeral. Chivalric imperatives permit the superimposition of order at the level of plot (through Theseus), and, correspondingly, by the Knight's intense need to control the narrative.

How does this rigorous control operate? The Knight works hard to suppress material that might contradict or problematize what he is currently relating. His is a strictly masculine world in which women spur men to heroic deeds. He recounts the exploits of Theseus winning Thebes, but sweeps aside the civilizing burial rites of the Theban widows, whose grief prompts Theseus's deposition of Creon, as too long to tell (1994). Equally, he refuses to tell how Emily and her sister were taken as prizes by Theseus in his battle with the Amazons at the start of the tale (875–92). The Knight's use of the rhetorical strategy of *occupatio* – telling us what he *won't* say – backfires because it hints at exactly what he aims to wipe out. It reminds us too of his struggle to keep control of a narrative that constantly threatens to burst its seams. We see this clearly at the end of the tale when he describes the funeral ceremony dedicated to Arcite. His constant repetition of 'Ne how' or 'Ne what' accumulates to articulate the negative or shadow side of this story. Beneath its order lies the potential for chaos. The Knight claims he will not tell how the grove is cleared ready for the funeral pyre, how the trees are felled, or how the gods run wildly around now that their habitat is destroyed and the birds and beasts flee. This is civilization stripped of its edifice of public display. Nor will he relate how the pyre is built, how Arcite is placed on it or what everyone does. Instead he ignores the intense emotion of the scene and the consequences of an epic, interventionist control (2919–66).

DISTORTING GENRE

The *Knight's Tale*, with its ideals of chivalry, also intersects those other romances of the *Tales*: the knights Palamon and Arcite recall, in different form, the rapist-knight of the *Wife of Bath's Tale* and echo Arveragus in the *Franklin's* as well as Sir Thopas. The story of *Sir Thopas* certainly falls into the same genre of romance. It lacks the epic status, the seriousness, even the length, of its parallel story the *Knight's Tale*. But it is replete with other clues to its generic patterning, directly mentioning the well-known romances of Hornchild, Guy of Warwick, Bevis of Hampton and, later, Sir Percival (VII, 897–900), and pointing towards other well-known medieval romance poems like *Sir Orfeo* and *Sir Launfal* (both of which involve fairy lovers) and the tales of Arthur and his Round Table knights. The poem calls on minstrels and storytellers to recount tales of romance and the joys of love (845) and highlights the popularity of the genre where men enjoy recounting other excellent romances (897).

Here we see some of the ways in which medieval story-telling is highly intertextual. A poem like *Sir Thopas* announces its genre through a series of clues, the employment of motifs, style and plot in ways highly similar to, in this instance, other romance stories. In this way, an audience comes to recognize and expect certain stock characters and resolutions. Yet Chaucer plays with these expectations to give us unexpected resonances such as those we have already explored in the tales of the Miller and the Knight. In this way, *Sir Thopas* can become, in part, a literary in-joke. Its humour derives precisely from audience expectation. Here the traditional love object is, unusually, not a real woman but an invisible fairy queen. In keeping with the central romance motif, this woman inspires Thopas's quest. Instead of rescuing her and taking her home to marry, he never even finds her. Equally, his confrontation with the giant who, according to generic convention, ought to be holding her captive, is one huge anticlimax. Thopas is far from being the classic dangerous man of daring deed, like the giant (809). He comes to fight without his armour; his claim to have left it behind justifies his fleeing home, apparently to collect it, for there is no knightly prowess in arms in *this* story, unlike the bitter physical rivalry of Palamon and Arcite in the *Knight's Tale*. The giant chucks stones at Thopas who beats a hasty retreat. Back home, he boasts of a three-headed giant and so exaggerates his own status as a romance hero similar to those of other stories invoked elsewhere in the poem. Thopas swears he will kill the giant. Not by the body of Christ as we might expect given the importance of this confrontation in the romance genre, but on ale and bread (872–3), a domestic image that thoroughly deflates this central motif.

Some critics suspect *Sir Thopas* is about the nature of poetry and its writing, an intertextual weaving in the medieval tradition of *auctoritas* that calls attention to the ways in which tales can intersect, undercut and work in dialogue with each other. *Sir Thopas* slips the constraints of genre to produce, depending on how we choose to read, a textual joke and/or questions about the nature and security of those gender norms apparently embedded in the romance genre. It is not simply that some pairs of tales – the *Miller's/Knight's* and *Miller's/Reeve's* – subvert each other. Rather, stories cut across the entire *Tales* to operate contingently throughout, in a manner recalling those who insist we read the *Tales* as a whole.

MARRIAGE AND SEXUALITY

When the Parson preaches against the sin of lechery, he links it
to the preservation of the sacrament of marriage. The institution
of marriage is embedded 'in paradys, in the estaat of innocence,
to multiplye mankynde to the service of God'. As such, fornication, prostitution, pimping, or other harlotry is a wrong done to
Christ who, it is said, owns us body and soul. The Parson
preaches that chastity – defined as cleanliness of heart, mind and
body – can be attained both in and out of marriage (X, 915). The
Parson tells us that a man must love his wife in moderation, as
though she is his sister, and second only to God (860). We know
that the medieval world deemed it sinful to engage in sex outside
marriage; even within it, the purpose of sex was clearly specified.
The Parson warns those married couples seeking only what he
terms fleshly delight that such pleasure is wrong (900–5). In marriage each partner's body was said to belong to the other so that
the three conditions of that union might be fulfilled. Sex, legiti-
mated only by marriage, was for procreation, the avoidance of
lust or fornication, and payment of the marital 'dette'. The
'dette' was a duty to yield up your body to the other, even if this
was against your inclination (935–41). Man must take only one
woman just as there is one Church and one God, something that,
as we shall see, proves problematical for those like the Wife of
Bath who take several partners in their lifetime (915–20). In a
lengthy and sometimes rambling *Prologue*, the Wife of Bath
rejects this notion of chastity. She tells us that she has married
five husbands and looks forward to the sixth (III, 44f–46).
Equally, her interpretation of St Paul's command of virginity is
that it is merely advice [conseille] not an instruction (61–70).
When Christ spoke of chastity or 'continence', she reasons, He
was addressing only those who would live perfect, saintly lives
(105–12), not ordinary people like herself.

The clash between the ideas of the Parson and the Wife is
important. The Parson supports his comments with a range of
written authorities like St Paul or St Augustine, plus biblical
precedents such as the story of the woman taken in adultery
(890/900/920/ 925/930). He appeals to a tradition involved in the

establishment of definitive truth. He acts within an institution (the Church itself) that is exceptionally powerful, one whose authority pervaded every aspect of the medieval world. Is it enough simply to have knowledge of these ideals? What effect did such notions have upon the lives of ordinary people? How might ideals have been put into practice?

The opening to the *Merchant's Tale* raises the question of the purpose of marriage when a 60-year-old bachelor decides it is time he wed. January offers a range of reasons supporting his decision. Marriage, he says, is a holy bond (IV, 1261) and a wife the best part of man's treasure (1270). He determines to choose a young woman on whom he might beget an heir (1270–721). January looks forward to a 'buxom' [obedient] wife (1287), one true and eager to care for him, to love and serve him till death (1286–92). Anticipating the joys of what he calls the yoke of marriage (1285), he asserts that a wife is a gift from God (1311) and describes marriage as a great sacrament (1319). The union is of one flesh (1335) with woman subservient to man. This is why, he reasons, God created Eve – to be a help-mate to man and a comfort to him (1324–31). She is made to work, keep house and do exactly as he requires without contradiction (1338–46).

January repeats what we already know from our earlier readings. What is important is that he convinces himself of the righteousness of marriage by quoting a range of authorities to justify his belief, including biblical 'good' women and philosophers like Seneca (1366–77). When January cites such written precedents, his words match the institutionalization of such authority seen in the *Parson's Tale*. Presumably, January's knowledge stems from reading and listening to clerical teaching. He claims that a wife is a gift from God (IV, 1311). He knows that other such gifts, like valuables, land or material objects, are from Fortune rather than heaven. Accordingly, they are subject to Fortune's vagaries and, as is the way of all earthly pleasures, cannot last. Yet January insists that the joy of a wife is eternal. In this way, then, he misreads clerical and Boethian teaching which privileges love of God (*caritas*) over love of earthly and transient things (*cupiditas*). January also informs May on their wedding night that he will perform at leisure, for their marriage legitimates such play;

as he puts it, a man can do no sin with his own wife or hurt himself with his own knife (1835–41).

These comments are in complete contrast to medieval ideals of behaviour concerning marriage and sexuality, as January himself knows full well. The Parson preaches that a man *can* hurt himself with his own knife (X, 855–6), while January's own explication of the purposes of sex in marriage is not entirely in keeping with Church teaching. He says that he is looking to marry in order to engender an heir and accurately cites the 'rules' on restrained sexuality and a brother–sister relationship between man and wife (1272/1446–55). But January misappropriates patristic and clerical authority to use it for his own ends. Experience tells him that older women are less inclined to be faithful than younger ones, which is why he seeks a woman under 20. He wants tender veal, he says, not old beef. Of course, January has been a bachelor until this moment and has pursued an active sex life throughout this time (1248–9); if anyone knows that young women are more receptive to teaching and moulding, it is surely him. In fact, even as he declares his awareness of the need for sexual moderation in keeping with medieval ideals, he boasts of his continued vigour and appetite, despite his 60 years and 'hoor' on his head (1457–66). In short, January admits he is definitely *not* planning to live chastely and moderately as Church teaching advocates.

Thus experience and personal inclination clash with abstract authority. Knowledge is open both to misreading and to manipulation, a form of 'glosynge' [glossing] we see the Wife of Bath engage in later. Through this juxtaposition, Chaucer is able to highlight a potential clash between written, clerical authority and everyday experience, a gap between the ideal (how we *ought* to live our lives) and ordinary practice (how we do live our lives). Even so, Chaucer invites us to laugh at the Wife's idiosyncratic vision of the world. Well versed in marriage, she admits to having chosen her husbands for both financial security and their 'nether purs' (she means the size of their genitals) (III, 446). Her coarse asides are highly entertaining. She makes frequent, if coy, reference to her '*bele chose*', '*quoniam*' or 'chambre of Venus'. The flaunting of her sexuality is more problematic. We may be shocked by her intimate confession of how she will freely use 'myn instrument' (149–50), boasting that her husband shall have it morning and night (152). She laughs when she recalls how she made her men work at night (201–2). She adds that she never loved in moderation but always followed her 'appetit', regardless of what the man looked like (622–5).

Her delight in the body might be read as an integral feature of a virago, the epitome of the very anti-feminist books she takes exception to Jankyn reading. She cheats, dresses up, gossips and answers back. Has Chaucer created a depraved monster, proof of women's 'known' treachery and insatiable sexual appetite? Or is she simply comic, not to be taken seriously? It is equally possible that Alison is, in fact, intended to invoke our compassion. Her innocent chatter hints at a longing for love. She likes any man so long as 'he liked me' (625) and cries 'Allas, allas! That evere love was synne!' (614). Yet she still chooses husbands for their wealth and equates sex with money. She argues that by playing hard to get women increase men's desire, just as a market shortage increases prices while a glut lowers them (522–3), and then takes Jankyn for love. Is Chaucer upholding the traditional division of women as whores or saints, the old Eve–Madonna split? Or is the picture more ambiguous than this?

In the *Merchant's Tale* a young girl is brought to bed as still as a stone (IV, 1818). This startling image recalls a medieval ideal of passive femininity taken to its extremes; it implies not simply reluctance, but a near-catatonic state that calls attention to the tyrannical force such ideals may exert. We may laugh at the description of old January's honeymoon lovemaking, but we are also repulsed by his concentration on his new bride, followed by his delighted air the next morning (1819–59). His appearance is more than off-putting with the slack skin of his neck wobbling as he sings. Even worse, the oppositional thinking that informs such regulations about medieval sexuality – the man as active, the woman passive – is here explored in telling detail. January's activities hint at if not rape, then a lack of mutual pleasure. Each time he looks on May, he is 'ravvyshed' in a trance (1750) and in his mind he begins to 'manace' or threaten her (1752). He imagines holding her in his arms harder than Paris ever did Helen

(1753–4), an allusion to the abduction of Helen of Troy, an image of forceful dominance intensified by the inclusion of the figures of Pluto and Proserpine in the tale (in classical myth, Proserpine was captured by Pluto and made to be his bride).

About May's response the text is tellingly silent. We assume she is simply the passive recipient of pleasure. In fact, significant breaks in the narration highlight some other crucial, underlying questions. The narrator – or is it Chaucer? – asks 'God woot' what May 'thoughte in hir/herte' when she saw January the morning after their wedding night. He adds, 'She preyseth nat his pleyyng worth a bene' (1851–4). Equally, when May is woken in the middle of the night and made to have sex with her husband, the narrator's own ambivalence is clear. He withdraws from the revelation of the full details and raises the question of whether May thought it all paradise or hell (1962–4).

EXEMPLARY MEN AND WOMEN

The *Parson's Tale* also informs us of a medieval ideal governing and circumscribing attitudes towards women. According to St Peter, a woman should be obedient to her husband or father, 'mesurable' in the way she looks and carries herself or behaves (laughing is to be discouraged), and discreet in all her words and deeds (935). She may well be admired for her beauty, but she must also be meek, mild, modest, patient and, preferably, silent in all things. Chaucer presents us with a handful of women in the *Tales* who are admired, apparently, for exactly this: Custance, Cecilia, Griselda and Virginia in the *Physician's Tale*. The cumulative irony of the epithet 'fresshe May' in the *Merchant's Tale* takes its effect, in part, from the repeated description of 'fresshe Emelye' in the *Knight's*, that epic story of love and chivalry. Emily is first spotted by Palamon and Arcite, while gathering flowers in the garden to make a garland for her long, braided hair. She sings like an angel as she celebrates Mayday. The Knight insists she is fairer than the lily and fresher than all the spring flowers she plucks. Like them, she too is all rosy and dewy. This is Emily the bright (I, 1737), her natural beauty enhanced by the apparently idyllic setting that frames her (I, 1034–55). But this idealized portrait is coloured by the knowledge that she is, in fact, a prisoner brought home as a trophy of war by Theseus when he conquers the realm of the Amazons and marries its queen, her sister Hippolyta.

As Emily walks, each step measures the constraints of a walled garden that abuts the tower in which Palamon and Arcite are imprisoned. Like them, she is a captive, a possession held by Theseus. Unlike them, she remains subject to the dominating and acquisitive gaze of both the knights who watch her from their prison cell and the narrator-Knight who offers her submissive example to the speculative eye of his audience.

Embedded within this ideal, then, is the 'natural' or taken-for-granted assumption that the female love object of stories such as this is a possession to be appropriated and circulated among men. Emily's movements are collated by the narrator and restrained by Theseus, who only later allows her out into the grove to observe the Mayday feast when he decides. The Knight repeatedly terms her 'my lady'. Palamon and Arcite fight over her like a dog over a bone. Arcite continually describes her as 'myn Emelye' during his death-bed scene, before finally giving her over to Palamon (1770–808). In the same way, Theseus calls her 'my sister' (1820/1833) and assumes the right to give her away to one of the knights, declaring Arcite can have her for he has 'ywonne' her, fair and square, in the lists (2659). At the end, Theseus hands her over to Palamon with 'my fulle assent', insisting she must take him for her husband and 'for lord' (3081), a transaction effected in formal language and backed by parliament in order to underscore the subservient ideal of womanhood that the tale seemingly propagates. In the same way, Theseus insists 'I speke as for my sister Emelye' (1833), thereby underscoring his right to deny her any power.

The extent of feminine power is further constrained by the implicit assumption that women disrupt fraternal chivalric bonds and, so, potentially damage the smooth operations of patriarchy. When Palamon and Arcite first see Emily they are injured by her beauty. Palamon cries 'Ah' as though stung to the heart and claims she has hurt him through the eye. Arcite insists that her appearance slays him (1077–9/1096/1118–19). Arcite's fatal accident is a freak event, yet the narrator contrives to make Emily responsible for it. Arcite looks up at her. Their eyes meet and, in an intensification of that first wounding sight of her, his horse starts and throws him (1676–99). Even as she quietly accepts Palamon as her husband at the end, Theseus reminds her that this is a king's son, one who 'had for yow so greet adversitee' (3087).

A passive, idealized Emily is, then, typically also a potential catalyst for chaos. This is the danger that necessitates and, further, legitimates that masculine 'maistrie' against which the Wife of Bath so vigorously kicks. So, the Knight affirms a marriage in which the bride is given away by a paternalistic and seemingly benevolent Theseus, the same man who captured her and took her, against her will, far from her home, there to wipe out all potential for transgression. Diana, goddess of chastity, has warned her that she must marry one of the cousins for this is masculine law, 'eterne word writen and confermed' (2350) which even Diana must recognize: and so, 'Thus endeth . . . Emelye' (3107). Her previous life – as an independent Amazon warrior-princess, armed with bow and arrow and also a lily, symbolic of the chastity to which she has dedicated her life – is erased.

If the Wife is a typical example of the unruly woman of anti-feminist literature, what are we to make of May's behaviour in the *Merchant's Tale*? For the Merchant, all is clear; in his misogynistic world, May exemplifies how women can never be trusted. But in the light of old January's avid and repellent pursuit of sexual delight with a girl he imagines as pliant as wax (IV, 1429–30), her switch from passive silence at the start of the tale to active defiance takes on especial resonance. May makes a wax imprint of the key to January's private 'Eden' in order to admit her lover into the garden (2116–24) and later follows Alison's advice to other women which is to speak boldly and accuse men of things they have never done (III, 226–28) and outdo them 'word for word' (see 419–22). So, too, the Wife's experience ensures 'maistrie' over men. By accusing her husbands of lechery, she is able to go out freely, even at night, all under the guise of searching out what she alleges are her husbands' partners in adultery (III, 397–8). She travels on pilgrimages or processions, attends weddings, plays, and parties

(555–9). The Wife dresses up in her finery (see 337–56) and, above all, demands the right to act 'at large', freely, and as she wishes (322).

Alison flaunts herself in defiance of medieval codes of behaviour for women. Does Chaucer intend us to take seriously her *Prologue*? What are we to make of her comments about sex? She acts the part of the grieving widow at her fourth husband's funeral because, she says, that is what wives are expected to do (558–89). In reality, she spends her time lusting after Jankyn their parish clerk, 20 years old to her 40 (596–601). In bed, she demands that her husbands make love to her, but feigns enjoyment revealing her dislike of old 'bacon' [flesh]. Her aim is 'wynnyng', to use sex to gain money in a manner that takes literally the notion of marital 'dette' (407–18). Alison teases them, nagging then kissing them, urging patience and falsely promising that her '*bele chose*' is for them alone (431–501). The Wife's portrait is a complex, contradictory one. Many twenty-first-century readers find her feisty, active defiance and manipulation of clerical and anti-feminist authorities highly appealing. It is important to remember that, despite this, her unruliness is condemned in those same writings. Nevertheless, her behaviour – and that of Alison in the *Miller's Tale* or May's – calls sharp attention to the nature of many medieval marriages where Church teachings emphasize its sacramental value and deny the possibility of love and enjoyment.

QUEER READINGS

What of medieval thinking about masculinity? Its medieval 'definition' associates it with mastery, power, rationality and abstract, intellectual thinking. Where the feminine is allied with the body or unruly flesh, masculinity is represented by the head, dominant over all and in charge of all physical and emotional faculties. To be masculine means to be active, competitive and on top, literally so in the case of sex. In short, men *do* and women wait.

Harry Bailly is remarkably tender about his reputation as a man's man, and with reason. Through a series of dramatic links, it emerges that he is afraid of his wife. He wishes that he had never married her, a confession he can only reveal in 'conseil' or private for fear it will get back to her (IV, 2431). Harry particularly admires the modest restraint of an ideal femininity he thinks he sees in tales like those from the Clerk, the Physician and in the *Melibee*. In contrast, his own wife is the voluble, nagging shrew of anti-feminist literature. She winds him up until he loses that masculine attribute of reason and becomes as wild and out of control as a lion (1916). She urges him to beat his servants harder, rages about the neighbours and demands he avenge all insults to her; until he does, she 'rampeth' in his face (1897–904). Harry fears that her constant verbal attacks – to which he responds equally madly – will end with him murdering someone, for he is 'perilous' with a knife in his hand (1919).

The comedy of Harry as a battered husband calls attention to constructions of masculinity in other ways. Harry's response to his wife shakes masculinity to its core. In the same way, his wife undermines his masculine 'self', calling him 'milksop' and 'coward ape' (1910). In response, he jokes about the imagined sexual potency of men like the Monk or the Nun's Priest (VII, 1941/VII, 3448). Masculinity defines itself through heterosexual display, joshing, swearing, and gambling (the story contest wager). Or does it? These gendered taunts make him especially sensitive to what is masculine in others and that which he himself might lack, contributing to Harry's over-performance or exaggeration of a version of masculinity he fears he cannot live up to; hence, his wife's dismissive comment that she will take his (phallic) knife and he can have her spinning wheel (VII, 1906–8). Harry's portrait is, then, an ambivalent version of masculinity. The category of 'masculine' slips its seemingly fixed parameters to remind us that it is an anxious, ill-defined state, one that means variously.

This enigma is intensified in the first tale that Chaucer-the-pilgrim relates. In *Sir Thopas*, masculinity presents as insecure, a constantly dissipating and challenged notion. As a masculine chivalric hero Thopas is immediately found wanting. This 'lack' is also exacerbated by the generic conventions of the romance tale in which he appears. As I suggested earlier, in order to achieve full adult knighthood the hero must defend his chivalric community of fellow knights, rescue and marry the girl and return home in glory. Physical prowess, fraternal camaraderie and a compulsive heterosexuality (seen in the way such stories end in marriage) drive these tales of chivalry. But Thopas fails on all counts, thus calling into question constructions of masculinity.

In appearance, Thopas seems rather effeminate, or at least androgynous (see VII, 724–47) in stark contrast to those descriptions of other knights like Palamon and Arcite, or Harry Bailly's imposing (if deceptive) physical presence. Instead, rather like the 'popet' Chaucer-the-pilgrim (VII, 701), he seems more like the usual female *object* of romance than its masculine subject. He wears fine linen, a costly silk robe, stockings from Bruges and shoes of Cordovan leather (725–35). Romance tales often elaborate, at length, an armouring scene as part of what constitutes masculine chivalry. Here the details are over the top, especially in view of the fact that Thopas's knightly credentials are never finally secured. His armour seems more decorative than functional; he even leaves it at home when facing the giant (819). On his helmet is a drawing of a lily (906–7) while his coat of arms is said to be as white as a lily (865–6). This persistent association with flowers (remember his lips like a rose) further feminizes him. Thopas seems to avoid sexual maturity, which is, in part, the function of the chivalric quest. The details of the lily remarked earlier are significant, for the lily symbolizes virginity. Other invocations of chastity compound his lack of masculine virility. Though many women seek him out, Thopas remains fresh as a dog-rose (745–6). His name derives from the gemstone topaz, said to fend off lust. Even Thopas's love object is an *invisible* elf-queen, physically absent from this quest.

Sir Thopas parodies a masculine, chivalric hero that we might set against other depictions in the *Tales*. In the *Knight's Tale*, both Palamon and Arcite have thickly bearded, manly faces. One is compared to a lion, the other to a griffin. Arcite's yellow hair glitters like the sun. Palamon's is as black as a raven's wing (I, 2128–81). These are images of hard strength, and also natural comparisons that suggest masculinity is contrived as easy or is a 'natural' attribute of their powerful knightly status. But how easy is it to distinguish Palamon and Arcite? The pair are always together, are imprisoned in the same cell and in love with the same woman. Their mothers are sisters and so the two are cousins (I, 1019). They are fellow Thebans and of royal blood. They are 'brothers-sworn' (1147/1161), blood brothers and brothers-in-arms. Whatever happens, they are fellow knights who, even as they prepare for combat with each other, still help the other to arm 'as he were his owene brother' (1652). Palamon and Arcite are thus closely related both by blood kinship and by the bonds of chivalry. Their twinning is a crucial part of this chivalric code where brother knights vow to die for each other and, as in the marriage service, promise to stay together till death (I, 1134). In many ways, the pair valorize masculine ties and assert masculinity. Even their rivalry over Emily is presented as a 'natural' or inevitable outcome of heterosexuality.

Yet something disturbs about this claustrophobic relationship where they seem more passionate about each other and their contest than about Emily herself. So closely connected are these two that they are found together on the battlefield wrapped in a seemingly loving embrace, 'Bothe in oone armes' (1012). Their later confrontation in the lists is also intensely physical, a close grappling and focus on bodily contact (echoed in the fighting of the rioters in the *Pardoner's Tale*) where 'In gooth' spurs, 'In gooth' spears right up to the hilt and opponents can feel the 'prikke' or thrust of a lance right to the breast bone (2600–6). It is certainly not unusual for medieval chivalric romance stories to describe battles in overtly sexual images, as here. It is a deliberate technique intended to enhance masculinity, despite its suggestions otherwise. But Chaucer's use of 'prikke' in the *Tales* is an unusual one interlaced across several stories. Its connotation in the *Reeve's Tale* is, for example, explicitly sexual; the Reeve tells how the student John leaps on top of the miller's wife while she sleeps and 'priketh hard and depe as he were mad' (I, 4229–31). Does this 'twinning' indicate that masculinity rests upon those homo-social bonds so conspicuously absent in the lone and dubious figuration of Chaucer-the-pilgrim, whose own story is that of a single, loveless knight frantically driving himself into a narrative impasse?

The singular figure of the Pardoner creates further ambivalences over the notion of masculinity. The Pardoner is the subject of intense critical scrutiny. Is he rampantly heterosexual yet somehow effeminate (a condition medieval minds believed to be the result of excessive sexual behaviours), rather like Sir Thopas or Absolon in the *Miller's Tale*? Is he homosexual, evidenced, in part, by his relationship with the Summoner? Is he a eunuch or somehow neither one sex nor the other? The *General Prologue* is distinctly unhelpful if we are looking to solve an enigma exacerbated by the Pardoner's self-fashioning in his own *Prologue*. There, his claims to have a pretty wench in every town (VI, 453), along with his later admission to the Wife of Bath that he was once going to marry (III, 187), seems to confirm a heterosexuality that is undercut elsewhere. A hint of depravity is also signed through the animal terminology that works to construct his portrait; even this is inconclusive in determining his gender and sexuality.

We are told that the Pardoner has a voice as small as a goat with its association both with hermaphrodites and lechery. In classical iconography, Lechery is sometimes personified as a man riding a goat (or else a woman riding one backwards, signal of her unnatural and perverse behaviour). Even as he *apparently* pursues women, the Pardoner retains a close friendship with the Summoner, himself replete with sexual and venereal images (see I, 623–35). The Pardoner sings 'Com hider love to me', while the Summoner bears him an ambiguously worded 'stif bourdon' (I, 672–3); does this mean he simply accompanies him on the bass line, or is it more sexually suggestive?

The possibility that the Pardoner is a eunuch or a hermaphrodite seems corroborated by the fact that he will never have a beard (I, 689) and, also, by his eyes which the narrator declares bulge like a hare's (684). Some classical and medieval texts indicate that the hare is hermaphroditic; others, that the males bear young in their wombs. Even more suggest that the hare grows a new anus each year, hence its connections to homosexuality. Chaucer-the-pilgrim's famous assertion, 'I trowe [think] he were a geldyng or a mare' (691), intensifies this conflicting perception. A gelding is, of course, a castrated horse and so seems to affirm that the

Pardoner's sexed body is not securely male. Yet the term 'mare' refers to both a female horse – thus pointing up the Pardoner's effeminacy – and a medieval colloquialism for the passive partner of male-to-male anal sexual intercourse. Thus the Pardoner is exceptionally difficult to classify. It is not *solving* the enigma that is important, but the enigma itself. Speculation about whether the Pardoner is or is not gay (a term probably illegible to a medieval world) is interesting (see Kruger 1994) but, ultimately, not quite the point, in my view. The Pardoner disturbs *precisely because* we can never be exactly sure of his masculinity, precisely because he is a gelding *or* a mare, an openness that doubly impacts when we revisit the Pardoner's confrontation with Harry Bailly.

The Pardoner carries a pouch, a 'male', that dangles down in his 'lappe' (I, 6861) to point towards the secret, possible lack of his male body. His relics are in this pouch, those papal bulls and patented letters authorizing his sale of pardons. These, say the Pardoner, are his 'warente', protection for the secrets of his occupation and warranty against any challenge to its authority (VI, 335–40). But these papal bulls seemingly pun on the 'coillons' or 'balls' he supposedly lacks, and to which Harry draws attention when he threatens to cut them off and carry them round as a relic to avenge the insult he believes the Pardoner gives him at the end of his story (VI, 954–5). In this respect, Harry Bailly's threat matches the Pardoner's command to Harry to unbuckle his purse (945), literally to offer money but implicitly to expose his genitalia, one proof of masculine identity. Note that both Harry and the Pardoner refuse to show each other this proof and to settle once and for all the issue of masculinity implicitly raised by their confrontation. Or, indeed, that of the homosexual desire also imputed by the Pardoner's invitation to unbuckle.

Harry Bailly attempts to assert his own masculinity and to refute the charge of homosexual desire by verbally emasculating the Pardoner. At the same time, through his contempt for relics both saintly and secular (the Pardoner's breeches), he denies the Pardoner's masculine authority invested in him by the Church. In turn, the Pardoner clings to the warranted authority of the documents in his pouch, those bulls/balls that have no real guarantee of meaning and, hence, can never be revealed openly. The confrontation ends, at the Knight's instigation, with the kiss of peace commonly recognized as a kiss of brotherhood and exchanged between monks. Yet far from restoring masculine authority and securely gendered status, the moment remains charged. The Knight asks the Pardoner to draw nearer and receive the kiss (VI, 964–8). This is almost an invitation to become the 'mare', the passive recipient of an only vaguely defined act. Rather than a signal of fraternal, Christian bonds, the intimacy of the kiss of peace may also be read as homoerotic. This allusion intensifies once we recall the numerous jokes circulating (and recorded) in the medieval world that suggested clerics and monks were notorious sodomites. Here, this incident, considered afresh, contributes to the failure of masculinity, and gender more generally, to define itself clearly in *The Canterbury Tales*.

The *Summoner's Tale* also explores these ideas. The Summoner tells of a 'lymtour', a travelling friar who arrives at the house of bedridden Thomas. The friar claims he needs Thomas's gold for the building of a church. Thomas tells the friar he has a little something for him and his brethren. He invites him to slide his hand down his back and feel around for his gift. There, he says, beneath 'my buttok' is something 'I have hyd in pryvetee' (2129–43). The friar duly gropes 'Aboute his tuwel' until suddenly Thomas 'leet the frere a fart', one louder than a horse (2145–51). Thus the empty, hollow sound of the friar's preaching is rewarded with the same, but these unsettling details of intimate, male-on-male touching hint at a queer reading of the tale.

KNOWLEDGE AND EXPERIENCE

When John agrees to build three separate boats in preparation for Noah's Flood and hang them from the rafters in the roof, we cannot believe his stupidity in falling for Nicholas's elaborate plan to 'swyve' his wife. But John's credulous gullibility rests on one thing: Nicholas's citation of authorities, both general and biblical, to 'prove' his warning of a second flood (I, 3504–7). Nicholas twice insists that this is all 'Goddes owene heeste [commandment] deere' (3588) and adds that he cannot explain it for

'I wol nat tellen Goddes pryvetee' (3558). Nicholas's superior knowledge is, thus, vested in Christian authority. Later, when Nicholas pretends to be in a trance, a worried John sends his servant to check on him. John fears that something is badly amiss for today he saw a body being carried into church. On the previous Monday he had seen with his own eyes that same man alive and at his work (3425–30). John is convinced of his premonition when the servant reports that Nicholas is sitting bolt upright in bed as if moon-struck. This, says John, is what happens to a man who meddles in astronomy. He argues that men should not seek to know of God's secrets and cites the example of a clerk's obsession with astronomy. The clerk walks the fields 'for to prye' upon the stars. He is so busy looking up to heaven that he fails to see the clay pit into which he subsequently falls (3457–61).

This entertaining interlude highlights not purely John's simple ignorance, but a clash between authority and experience. John relies upon what he can actually see with his own eyes as evidence of authority and truth. He witnesses a man drop dead – a premonition of disaster – plus a crazed Nicholas entranced in his bed and a man fall into a pit, all proof of the dangers of studying. Here Chaucer calls into question the nature of knowledge. In what can we trust? Our experience? Our faith in the unseen, in God? Do we accept the evidence of our own eyes, or what others – books, clerics, the Church – tell us? Are these authorities inviolable or can they be glossed differently, misappropriated for personal gain and/or opened up to different perspectives? These are the problems to which we are returned time and again.

The Wife of Bath's fight with her beloved fifth husband, the clerk Jankyn, is born of a frustrated desire to confront an authoritative tradition that rejects women as inferior and dangerous beings. At first glance, their struggle appears to return us to a notion of 'maistrie' idealized in the *Franklin's Tale*. She tells us that Jankyn beats her (III, 505–7/511), blows she will feel on her ribs as long as she lives. Yet, she loves him best of all (512–13). Once, he punched her on the ear, leaving her deaf (634–6), but, in return, she refuses to be silent or kept in. When she describes their battle, it ends with her insistence that 'He yaf me al the bridel in myn hond' (813) and 'al the soveraynetee' (818). What angers the Wife is Jankyn's insistence upon reading a collection of anti-feminist tracts by writers such as Valerius, Theofrastus, St Jerome, Tertullian and a host of other patristic authorities (671–81). These works are all bound in one volume, a detail that signifies their insistent, reductive typecasting of 'woman' as a sinner, and reading them is Jankyn's favourite occupation. Their battle commences when Alison rips out three pages of his book and punches him in the face (788–93), action symbolic of a declared war of the sexes and an attempt for a woman to make her voice heard. Her provocation has been intense. Jankyn repeats an array of tales: of Eve taking the apple so that woman is the ruin of all mankind; of treacherous women like Delilah, Amphiorax, Livia and Lucia; and so on (713–71). Finally, he cites numerous proverbs about women's nagging, anger and voracious lust (773–85).

This is the background against which the entire *Prologue* is set. As fast as Chaucer proposes the Wife as an example of a potential rebel (albeit a humorous one), he simultaneously reminds us of the rules against which she is judged and found wanting. When she assaults her husband, she strikes a blow against that authority – not simply against traditional domination in marriage, but what these books represent, a gold standard for wifely behaviour. So, when she tears up his book and hits him, her actions directly challenge an authoritative tradition that damns her whether she behaves correctly or not. Similarly, the *Wife of Bath's Prologue* begins by raising a series of questions about the undisputed authority not only of Church teaching but of the written word itself. Alison begins by commenting upon the technique of 'glosyng', where male clerics and other writers offer commentaries upon and interpretations of the Bible. It is a process that leads to definitive statements about Christ's intentions or meaning. This, in turn, permits the establishment of ideals governing belief and behaviour, some of which I have explored throughout this book. Thus Alison's remarks bring into sharp focus some fundamental tenets of medieval life.

Alison's remark – that though men may conjecture and 'glose', no one can ever finally say what is true – fractures the notion of definitive proof which authority was intended to provide. If the

Bible provides written evidence, then it is, according to Alison, both contradictory and impractical. It cites virginity as exemplary, yet tells us to wax and multiply (28) and to leave our mothers and marry. Equally, she says, Christ nowhere actually specifies the number of marriages that are lawful (32). Elsewhere, Dorigen, in the *Franklin's Tale*, recognizes that her only role model is the wife or maid who will kill herself rather than suffer the shame of sexual dishonour. She quotes 'ensamples' at tedious length (V, 1355–456), but none solves the dilemma of her promise to Aurelius.

There are gaps in any written tradition that demand interpretation – hence, the practice of 'glosyng'. Yet that same practice can never finally agree *because* of those gaps. That very ambiguity means that the Wife of Bath can rebel against masculine 'truth' to provide an alternative version that nevertheless remains deeply implicated in the very process she struggles against. So, she challenges written and clerical authority by inverting the usual process of defining it, instead taking her lived experience and 'matching' it against a citation, rather than using the ideal or the citation as an example of how to live. Yet, her *Prologue* retains the classic question-and-answer form of masculine debate, while every detail of her advice on how to live that alternative life conforms to anti-feminist literature *and* to literary typology (that of the sexually corrupt Old Woman instructing others in depravity).

Authority of experience is also what the god Pluto seems to confirm towards the end of the *Merchant's Tale*, as he and Proserpine observe May's treachery in January's walled garden. It is experience, Pluto reasons, that daily proves the many treasons done to man by women. Yet the examples he cites as evidence are taken not from life, but from ten hundred thousand tales, the words of Solomon who can find no praiseworthy women, or Jesus Syrak, author of *Eccliesiasticus* (IV, 2237–75). The visual evidence of May's planned trickery of blind January confirms Pluto's reading, as, suddenly, knowledge (from books *and* life) comes together. Thus he swears to grant January the return of his sight so that he can have material proof of her wickedness (2,251–63). The situation is made more complex, however, by Proserpine's challenge to her consort. She argues that women's boldness enables them to face down and contradict all that men see with their eyes (2264–75). She implies that since men say women are 'jangleresses', or chatterboxes (2307), they might as well live up to it and use their superior verbal dexterity to outwit men. This is the gift that she, in her turn, grants to May (2305–9). In addition, she refutes Pluto's knowledge by dismissing the authorities he relies upon to offer, instead, alternative readings (2277–300). She asks, why should she care for any man's authorities (2277)? Like the Wife of Bath, she rejects entirely the villainy of such books written about women as not worth 'a boterflye!' (2304).

Once again this quarrel opens up a series of questions about the reliability of traditionally authoritative sources. Written authority becomes a matter of interpreting a range of references that may be ambiguous or contradictory. Experiential knowledge (what you know or see from life) is, interestingly, no more reliable either, just as the Pardoner's tangible relics are fake. Despite the evidence of his eyes, January is deceived by May's glossing of her behaviour. January claims he saw that Damyan 'swyved thee' (2378). May insists that he saw imperfectly, for sight returned so suddenly needs time to adjust (2395–406). Crucially it is 'glosyng' or interpretation that wins the day and denies the facts. The ending of the *Merchant's Tale* returns us to January's glossing of the marriage debate argued by his friends Justinius and Placebo at the start of the tale (IV, 1478–565/1655–88). January's insistence on the sacrament of marriage as the union of 'one flesh' (IV, 1331–5) conceals his desire to have only 'tendre veal' to satisfy his sexual urges (1415–30) and contradicts his later dismissal of written authority in favour of personal experience: 'Straw for thy Senek, and for thy proverbes!' (1567). Yet when January ignores Justinius's reminder that the Wife of Bath's 'confessions' have just confirmed the personal nightmare that lies in store (IV, 1685–7), we see how he twists authority simply to suit himself. So, too, the Pardoner's revelation that he abuses his office when he declares that souls can pick blackberries for all he cares: 'myn entente is nat but for to wynne/And nothing for correccioun of synne' (VI, 403–6).

Here, Chaucer undermines the very notion of authority by drawing our attention to what it conceals or (deliberately?) misreads. The *Tales* continually suggests that opinions are formed by listening to the authoritative and idealized comments of others *and* on the basis of practical, lived experience. The Wife of Bath demands to know why her perspective is any less powerful or 'correct' than any other. Her beliefs are juxtaposed with those of others: the Franklin's idealistic vision of equality; the Pardoner's self-confessed manipulation of an authority he relies upon for financial reward; John the carpenter's faith in the tangible world he inhabits as ultimate proof of knowledge; and so on.

ENDINGS AND CLOSURES

If Chaucer's work elides definitive answers and resists closure, what effect might this have upon the endings of his tales? Every story anticipates some kind of logical outcome to its plot, even a twist in its tail, or else a neat tying up of its narrative threads. A medieval audience would probably have expected 'sentence' – knowledge in the form of moral resolution or a clear, doctrinal message. Often we also seek emotional satisfaction, an ending that commands attention and matches the tone or tenor of the story it concludes. Yet Chaucer seemingly neglects to provide us with any of these, at least unless we all read in the literal way that Harry Bailly does. In part, this may be due to the pervasive influence of oral story form upon those early ventures into print. Some oral performances are likely to have been interrupted or suspended as part of a continuing saga, or left open deliberately in order to invite audience participation. Even so, Chaucer is unusual in his apparent inability either to close his narratives at all, or else to end them successfully in the sense of a fitting or necessary plot outcome. Other endings sometimes appear unsatisfactory: rushed, too neat or happy in contrast to the resonance of the tale, or an imposition that clearly intends to suppress certain elements but in so doing calls attention to them.

This refusal to provide easy answers or to resolve the many conflicts, tensions and ambiguities the poems raise is encapsulated in *The Canterbury Tales* itself. The *Tales* comes to us incomplete, in ten fragments and without a central organizing schema. Some of the difficulties of this includes the problem of its own ending: the *Parson's Tale* or the *Retraction*? Both invite a moral re-reading of a poem where no single viewpoint has been allowed to dominate, and authority – whether an abstract issue or Harry Bailly's dramatic authority – is continually tested. What if there is no end? After all, the pilgrims never actually reach Canterbury. These instances evidence an ongoing concern about the circulation of texts which must by their very nature always remain open, where stories veer away from authorial control and are variously replicated. In the concluding lines of *Troilus and Criseyde*, the narrator highlights the persistent concern of any medieval author over the reception of his work. He worries that once complete, it is now out of his control. It must suffer the fate of all poetry which is to be judged and interpreted, even misread. He can only hope that it will stand the test of time alongside other works (*T and C, V*, 1786–98). In this way, all endings are then but new beginnings, as well as continuations and alternative versions of other stories, themselves never finished, never dead. Even stories that end successfully invoke these anxieties, not least because all medieval tales point in the direction of other versions.

How, then, do these anxieties surface in *The Canterbury Tales*? Several stories fail to conclude at all, while others provide dubious or unsatisfactory endings. The *Cook's Tale* simply stops, apparently nowhere near any outcome at all (I, 4422). Only two lines into its third part, in mid-sentence description of some epic battles, the *Squire's Tale* runs out of steam. The Knight interrupts the *Monk's Tale*, explicitly condemning its lack of entertainment, something with which Harry Bailly agrees (VII, 2767–97). Perhaps the most famous interruption of all is to Chaucer-the-pilgrim's *Tale of Sir Thopas*. The story is marked by two corresponding yet paradoxical pairs of movement: inflation/contraction and mobility/stasis. Each of these works simultaneously to bear on the tale's structure and, consequently, its ending. On the one hand, Thopas is characterized by a mad 'prykkyng' whereby he rides round the countryside on a wild goose chase looking for his lady love. On the other, there are moments of complete immobility. He sits down on the grass, his meeting with the giant lacks action, and back home in the castle his life is sedentary, composed of idle feasting and boasting about his exploits. Equally, the text seemingly and comically inflates. Thopas faces a giant, the enormous Sir Elephant. His own credentials are blown up so that he is compared to other romance heroes like Guy of Warwick or Sir Percival. The incident with the giant is also exaggerated with Thopas bragging about his defeat of a three-headed monster (842/873). But again there is simultaneous contraction. Thopas is depicted as dainty, somewhat effeminate, with lips red as a rose, a little nose and fancy shoes and clothes (724–35). There is also an obvious diminution in terms of structure. The number of verses in each section is halved each time: eighteen to nine to four and a half (see Cohen 1999).

Many modern critics believe the text's only logical outcome is its disappearance. Even without Harry's interruption, it seems that the dialectics *Sir Thopas* invokes (mobility/stasis and inflation/contraction) can never be resolved. *Sir Thopas* is programmed to fizzle out, just as Thopas's quest will remain forever unfulfilled. Once again it terminates with a mid-sentence interruption, this time from Harry Bailly. He complains that such 'crap' rhymes hurt his ears (VII, 923). In this sense, the poem becomes a narrative impossibility, a hilarious example of irresolution and what happens when a genre is so twisted out of shape (in this case, a romance anticipating marriage as its outcome) that its very thwarting testifies to the precarious nature of its ideals in the first place. So, *Sir Thopas* is halted. Or is it? For there is that all-important little dash, its 'Til on a day –' (918) pointing onward, as yet another story circulates out into open space.

Rather than resolving issues, Chaucer's endings – and their bearing upon previous events – frequently open up further debate even as, in terms of plot, the story seems to fold entirely neatly. The tales of the Knight, the Clerk and the Miller exemplify this technique by suppressing elements of the narrative that otherwise disturb us. In the *Knight's Tale*, Theseus's concluding tournament – in which Palamon and Arcite fight for Emily's hand in marriage – is intended to restore order after the uncivilized chaos prompted by the pair's rivalry. Theseus uses the public occasion of the lists to channel safely the savage aggression witnessed when the two are caught fighting in the grove. The tournament is a mechanism designed to bring both personal and social resolution and order. Arcite's accidental death is only a temporary interruption to this plan. It is quickly followed by Theseus's 'bisy cure' (I, 2853) in the form of a lavish state funeral, a palliative for the shock and grief of the city. After a suitable period of mourning, Theseus hands over Emily to Palamon in a compensatory gesture that affirms notions of patriarchal privilege with the ideal union of husband and wife. Though the story closes down, there remains in the minds of many readers a deep disquiet. Emily fails to preserve the liberty she prayed for, and Palamon's best friend and brother-in-arms dies. Such unsettling losses are evident in the language employed to describe their union. Theirs is a marriage said to be without words of jealousy or other vexation (3105–6). With Emily, Palamon is tender (3103). Testament to a mature love that has withstood time and tragedy? Or suspiciously platonic and passionless, especially set against the heightened emotion of the knights' first encounter with Emily and the way Palamon *howls* at Arcite's death (2817), an immeasurably emotional response that renders his tenderness for Emily insipid?

Here the ending seems as much an imposition as those social and civic rules governing personal, everyday life. Rather than a nostalgic portrait of a dying golden age, the *Knight's Tale* seems to invite reflection upon the mechanisms of order in Chaucer's own time. It points to a gap between abstract ideals and lived reality similarly encountered in the fairy-tale conclusion tacked onto the debate about marriage, sexuality and masculine authority invigorated later in the *Wife of Bath's Prologue*. Viewed in this light, the ending of the *Knight's Tale*, as with *Sir Thopas*, is a logical and fitting outcome. Yet all the time it invites us to reconsider the tale and to read its darker, more hidden meanings rather than settle for the happy-ever-after the conclusion seemingly settles for.

So far, I have considered only incomplete, rushed or 'impossible' endings. What of those perfectly executed ones? Even these may not always be what they seem. The rousing end of the

Miller's Tale is typical of *fabliau* plot, where old men are always punished for their jealousy and the crime of marrying a young woman. She, on the other hand, invariably escapes scot-free after her adulterous fun, 'swyved' by one man and kissed on the 'nether' eye by another (I, 3850–2). Everyone laughs at John whose gullibility becomes a narrative in itself, a joke circulated throughout the community. Taken as a funny story, the conclusion seems entirely fitting.

But it is all too easy to dismiss the poem in this way. Rather, its neat conclusion, once again, perpetuates ambiguities raised elsewhere in the text's action and details. Several critics, even feminist ones (most famously, Hansen 1992), point to the final reference to Alison as 'this milleris wyf' (I, 3850). Here Alison suddenly reverts to the position of object, both of the verb and as her husband's possession. This disappearance into a narrative hole signifies that agency is returned to its 'rightful' place, back to the masculine. Yet the question of whether Alison, or the feminine, triumphs persists. A retrospective reading might argue that the ending is a gloss. It erases the fact that she instigates the misdirected kiss joke at the window in an answering-back to a masculine ideology that seeks to contain her. So, as we saw earlier, she directs Absolon away from his intended target – her body – and slams shut the window to deny him further access to her. Remember her self-satisfied 'Tee-hee!' (see 3721–41). The construction of gender is made even more problematic once Nicholas seizes the opportunity to share in the joke and substitutes his own body for Alison's. His subsequent branding by a hot 'kultour' is a phallic inscription; not on a female body, as we might expect, but on a male one as two men 'kiss'. The ambiguous desires and slippery notions of the *Miller's Tale* remain far more complex and unresolved than its final harmony might suggest.

So too, the narrator's concluding 'this tale is doon' and the thumping rhyme of 'rowte' and 'towte' (3853–4) emphatically close down discussion. But we are left with the problem of laughter. Is this a satisfactory communal laughter born of 'carnival'? In carnival, scatalogical and irreverent fun offers a ritualized space for a disruption that is only ever *licensed* misrule, and so always reaffirms the very order it seems to strain against. What kind of humour is this? At whose expense is the joke? John's for being foolish? Nicholas's for getting caught out? Absolon for his pretensions? Or Alison for being the joke all men share about women's 'pryvetee' or sex? Is this tale, finally, even funny at all? After all, it involves public and private humiliations, broken vows and an arm, badly burnt buttocks and an ambiguous but decidedly vicious attempt to assault someone with the red hot blade of a plough share. Who was the actual target of this attack? Alison? Where exactly on the body was it aimed? How exactly would it be deployed?

In these resounding questions, we see not resolution but a potential revolution: in reading and interpreting, in that open community of texts, audiences and the contingent discourses of those other medieval institutions like the Church or legal, scientific, political and medical 'knowledges' that invariably impinge upon how texts make meaning. In this way open endings become part of a medieval textual web whereby stories veer away from authorial control. Even the most resolute endings often force us to reconsider preceding events, or a tale's structure. They also open up to further debate a tale's ideals and issues, while often working against the grain of generic expectations or analogues (other versions of the tale).

DISCUSSION QUESTIONS

Narrative Voices
1. What, if any, problems arise from the role or stance of the fictional narrator of any work you have read?
2. Do you think there is anything to be gained by exploring the relationship between teller and tale?
3. Do you agree with the view that *The Canterbury Tales* needs to be looked at as a whole, or is it sufficient to read the tales divorced from their wider context?

Gender
1. Do you think that Chaucer could be described as a friend to women, or one sympathetic to their situation?

2. Are Chaucer's women abhorrent to a contemporary audience, and, if so, how might this impact upon our readings?
3. How much substance is there, do you think, in feminist readings of Chaucer's work?
4. In what ways might issues about gender impact upon our understanding of a medieval text like Chaucer's?
5. Do these gendered readings – masculine, feminist, or 'beyond gender' like queer – ultimately reinforce, rather than subvert, conventional and oppositional ways of constructing our world?

Authority and Experience
1. Why do you think that so much of *The Canterbury Tales* refuses final answers or definitions?
2. Do you agree that the *Tales* is a postmodern work, in that ultimately there is no authority to be found there?
3. Is Chaucer a subversive or radical writer in your view? Do his poems challenge fundamental notions of medieval existence, or is he finally on the side of received wisdom and order?

Endings
1. Do you agree that some endings offer a retrospective through which to re-read a tale?
2. Is it fair to say that happy endings in Chaucer are not always quite what they seem?
3. What, in your view, is the effect of avoiding closure?

CHAPTER 4

CRITICAL RECEPTION AND PUBLISHING HISTORY

However, or, perhaps, precisely *because* it is anathema to contemporary ideas about literature, we persist in searching for a stable, authoritative version of *The Canterbury Tales* probably unknown to a fourteenth-century audience. No manuscript of Chaucer's works survives from the period prior to his death in 1400. It may even be that the incomplete works – *House of Fame*, *The Legend of Good Women* and the *Tales* itself – were not actually published at all during Chaucer's lifetime. But those early compilers, such as his son Thomas, did such a good job after it that 82 manuscripts survive, at least in part, from the early years after Chaucer died. Often, the poem was not even printed as a whole; certainly, several stories seem to have lived independently of the *Tales*, circulated either singly or else as a loosely connected group. Pieces of *The Canterbury Tales* remain to us in numerous manuscript miscellanies, existing alongside sermons, prayers, other stories, recipes, and even a remedy for toothache. It seems there is no more a final, static version of the *Tales* than there was a stable canon of Chaucer's works, not least because medieval notions of authorship and textual authority were substantially different from ours. I return to a discussion of this expanded, and often falsely ascribed, Chaucer canon in the next section but it is important to note here that the Chaucerian apocrypha, as these spurious works are called, and the composition of the early folios, have a profound impact upon readership and critical reception.

Equally important is the social and political context inspiring their production. Chaucer's work was continually in print throughout Tudor times. In some respects, Chaucer was viewed as inspirational, a 'father' to other writers of vernacular works. This elevation of his status corresponds to an intense scrutiny of him as a *man*. A sixteenth-century 'Chaucer' is at once a conservative, a moralist harking back to a nostalgic vision of a feudal past, a nationalistic (because he writes in English) and anti-ecclesiastical royalist, and a man of great learning and scientific knowledge. Such a mix undoubtedly appealed to radicals and Protestant reformers, and is reflected in several formative folio compilations. William Thynne, producing editions in 1532, 1542 and 1551, marketed what he called the complete works of Geoffrey Chaucer. He includes 25 spurious works. The Chaucer he presents is a courtly poet, pro-monarchy and a defender of women. John Stowe (1561) reproduces Thynne's collection and adds another 18 poems, seven of them apocryphal. His Chaucer is heavily satirical and focused on sexual politics. The extra seven 'new' poems mock women and love, in accordance with the fashion of the time, to offer an anti-feminist Chaucer in contrast to the tone of Thynne's collections. Later, Thomas Speght (1598, 1602, 1687) edits a Chaucer that has fewer spurious poems than the others but is notable for its distinctive flavour. Speght returns to a more genial and courtly Chaucer. He grounds his choices in a framework that highlights Chaucer's royal connections through his close association with the Lancastrian house of John of Gaunt. This is, thus, the first time that the *Book of the Duchess*, allegedly an elegy to Gaunt's dead wife, appears in a folio edition (1598). As a result, Chaucer remains firmly associated with a reforming, Protestant, nationalistic enterprise and so we see the important inclusion of an apocryphal anti-clerical satire called *Jack Upland*.

The sixteenth-century folio editions of Chaucer give us a strong sense of an author who is an astute political commentator, deeply implicated in the construction of an emerging national identity. This undoubtedly sold books and elevated Chaucer's reputation. But to stress 'the man' seems directly opposed to a late-medieval understanding of authorship with its continual disappearance of 'author'. In fact, it remains a classic example of the centrality of audience and reader-response in the reception of medieval literary texts. By the time of John Urry's edition of Chaucer in 1721, the focus had switched away from political and social concerns and onto narrative. Urry attempts to resolve anxieties about the incomplete story-frame of *The Canterbury Tales* by offering two spurious 'second' tales, one allegedly from the Merchant (*Tale of Beryn*), and another from the Cook (*Tale of Gamelyn*). He also includes the *Retraction* as an end-piece to the collection for the first time since 1526, when it appeared in a compilation by Richard Pynson and then disappeared from the archives.

CRITICAL RECEPTION

If Chaucer is alive anywhere in contemporary society, it is surely in academia with its focus on teaching and learning, and its contigent market of study guides, student-friendly editions of the text and those publications of critical analysis upon which all academic essays must rest. It is here that we can begin to access Chaucer's critical reception. In so doing, it is important to ask to what extent is our response to Chaucer conditioned by what we read (and are compelled to reference) in academic commentaries, in a process not completely dissimilar from medieval textuality? How does this dynamic construct the Chaucer we recognize today? And how are we as readers and/or students to negotiate the huge and varied critical field within which the influential academy demands we position ourselves and our responses to Chaucer's texts?

In an attempt to guide you through some complex and competing ideas, I intend to isolate some specific fields of criticism/ individual critics who, for one reason or another, have influenced the changing world of Chaucer Studies. Any overview of critical interpretation brings its own dangers. It is certainly possible to identify and generalize about trends in criticism. Equally, some scholars are easily associated with particular critical fields or areas of enquiry. But these fields themselves are neither discrete nor stable. Nor have they emerged, as might seem to be the case in any survey of them, in any linear or chronological way. Rather, later developments in thinking often return to and redefine (sometimes radically) earlier fields, or else generate in parallel with each other. While it may be a useful shorthand to label a critic as, say, a gender theorist or a New Historicist, such categorizations may be too narrow. A single critical field may incorporate academics and writers who are as much marked by the *differences* between them as their similarities. Criticism is also subject to changing fashions and trends, including resistance to certain forms (generally, Chaucer Studies lagged behind other literary fields with regard to theory, adhering instead to a scholarship reliant on manuscripts and editing).

All criticism is thus energized by intersection and overlap. An individual theoretical field may hold within it many independent lines of investigation and is perhaps better discussed in terms of its plurality and interrelation; feminisms, not feminism, for example. In reading criticism, we need to be aware of it as a web of connections and contingencies. So, we cannot read one without the others, even if we finally choose to emphasize a particular interpretation or theoretical influence. In this way we demonstrate academic research skills by negotiating these areas and referring back to them in order to ground our own thinking and lend it authority. We bring together both textual analysis and our responses to critical commentaries in an effort to confront received interpretation *and* generate fresh insights.

TALKING HEADS

Though Kittredge wrote as long ago as 1915, his perspective on *The Canterbury Tales* retains a firm grip on Chaucer Studies in certain quarters. Most notably, some examination questions or assignment topics implicitly suggest a consistent match between speaker and story. Kittredge viewed the *Tales* primarily as a group of realistic characters participating in a story contest. As such, each figure becomes a modern-day 'talking head'. Their individual tales are dramatic monologues revelatory of 'self', with an internal logic and psychological consistency all of their own. This psychological realism is further enhanced when the Canterbury pilgrims engage the interactive drama of the storytelling frame. So, the speakers respond to each other and their stories in such a way that their realism becomes embedded. At the same time, this continual cross-response enables us to decide on the content and order of the various fragments of the *Tales*. For example, Kittredge identifies several tales that he unifies as the 'Marriage Group' on the basis of both the stories told and the interaction between the Wife, the Clerk, the Merchant and the Franklin, each with contradictory views on the subject of wedded bliss.

The appeal of Kittredge's reading is apparent in his pervasive influence. His is an early, and laudable attempt to negotiate both the polyvocal (competing voices) nature of the *Tales* and its intratextual (reading in and between stories), if fragmentary, force. Thus we are continually invited to read the tales together, to read across and within the whole poem in correspondence with the paradoxical notion of 'quiting'. For an example of this, look at the tales of the Knight, the Miller and the Reeve and the dramatic links that bind them.

Despite this, such readings perhaps work best with individual, stand-alone tales (hence its persistence on some school and college examination papers), for the weaknesses of Kittredge's approach are several and varied. A reading of this type is based solely upon the order of the *Tales* suggested in the Ellesmere manuscript, itself the basis of the modern *Riverside* edition. This ignores the existence of other manuscripts with a different order. Since all critics need a standard edition acceptable to most from which to work their critical interpretations, this might seem largely uncontroversial. Except that Kittredge's ideas rely on an order pre-conceived by Chaucer, an authoritative authorial intention that we now realize is difficult to recover. Once we change the pattern of the *Tales*, a possibility suggested by the existence of other editions, then the notion of thematic unity upon which Kittredge also depends is diminished. If we read more randomly, not even from start to finish, we multiply possibilities for reading across the stories and regroup them in different ways. Instead of the Wife of Bath as part of a 'Marriage Group', we might read her in conjunction with the Pardoner, for example, to connect up issues such as the authorization of speech, monstrous bodies and gendered identities.

Kittredge's insistence on psychologically real drama also over-looks some important facts about medieval narrative. For Chaucer, the dramatic frame is only a partial structuring device, one that moves in and out of view and neither offers closure to the poem, in the form of a return journey to Southwark, nor places limits upon its unfolding. Some figures who appear in the *General Prologue* line-up never tell a tale; others who are 'new' to the pilgrimage, such as the Canon's Yeoman, do. There is not always a clear motivation for the teller to recount the tale he/she does, especially when some stories seem to have been re-allocated to speakers (Wife from the *Shipman's Tale* to her own). Thus there is not always a 'best fit' between tale and teller, or even a consistent drama. Psychological realism is equally contestable, with the Wife of Bath a prime example. Hers is a typically com-posite figure partially taken from literature elsewhere as an example of a particular vice. She is also constructed through a particular narrative form (that of the question-and-answer debate of clerical works and sermons), and inconsistent or con-tradictory details. In this way, she can never be the three-dimen-sional, psychologically consistent 'character' necessary for a successful 'talking head'.

READING IN CONTEXT: DEFINITIONS OF HISTORY

Some theoretical fields insist that all literary texts must be placed within a historical and social framework, however difficult this retrospective might be. It is certainly true that to neglect the pro-found impact and dominating force of the medieval Church when reading Chaucer will severely restrict our interpretations. It is similarly dangerous to impose our own contemporary values on a 600-year-old poem. To insist that the Wife of Bath is an early proto-feminist (which she may be), without either acknowledging our own vested interests or taking into account other sources, issues and non-literary texts, many of them anti-feminist, devalues the productive potential of such an enterprise.

Yet the social context of a literary piece affects it in different ways. To privilege its importance is to privilege authorial inten-tion at the same time, not least by assuming an author will either produce a text that is a product of his/her context, or one that somehow reacts against it. Neither may be the case, as we shall see later. Equally, it presupposes that this context is easily retrievable from history. There is a danger that we view 'history' as a set of discrete, recoverable 'facts'. Such a perspective allows us to extrapolate a single unified culture known as 'medieval' and to mark it off from the present day. This 'pre-modern' context helps to form our own, but remains apart and other to it. As a definition it is contestable, not least in its assumption that history is both chronological and progressive.

Such a historical perspective informed the school of thought that dominated Chaucer Studies from the 1960s to the late 1980s. Its leading advocate was D. W. Robertson. The Robertsonian view of history as a stable entity apparently enabled its followers to uncover a medieval literary theory (which *was* in existence) and present it as the *only* way in which Chaucer's texts would have been received and understood. Robertson insists that all readings of medieval literature must be based on 'doctrine' or education. In other words, texts are allegorical in nature. They demand Christian exegesis, or explanation, in accordance with an individual moral message that sees the Wife and the Pardoner, for example, condemned by a medieval audience, and all women offered as examples of either Eve or Madonna and responded to accordingly. The model for such thinking depends, in part, upon St Augustine's insistence that we turn away from worldly things like sexual love, or attachment to people or possessions. Love of this type was known as *cupiditas*. In contrast, St Augustine advised us to look to God and heaven and to pursue *caritas*, a divine, 'disinterested' and pure love. A Robertsonian allegorical approach seeks close attention to small details or word meanings, as well as a focus upon plot outcomes, and takes into account inflections and names. The overwhelming force of these connections can, at times, persuade, but, once more, there are some inherent difficulties.

Again, this field relies upon strict adherence to the Ellesmere order of the *Tales* with the Parson as the authoritative, final Christian word and a *Retraction* that emphasizes contrition and disowns all 'immoral' works. But if we re-order the poems or read flexibly so that, as some have recently suggested, what is last is read first, then our perspective alters. For example, we receive the hint of a return journey, emphasizing not a preparation for heaven but a move back to the world and its affairs. Some also argue that since it was entirely usual to read allegorically in medieval culture, the *Retraction* is redundant, a recanting of immorality that is unnecessary or merely a conventional 'end' device. The Robertsonian school also narrows readings to present a resolutely one-dimensional answer to the many ambiguities integral to Chaucer's work. Such a view leads to a *Miller's Tale* that can only condemn sexual sin and adultery, and ignores the many questions raised by its apparently resolute ending. And what might it say of a tale like *Sir Thopas*?

RETHINKING HISTORY

The notion of history as a stable entity has been heavily challenged in Chaucer Studies, as it has been elsewhere. Some argue that history is not monolithic or even linear in its manifestation – instead, it is discontinuous. It tracks back and forth, across and between, to intersect our own time as well as others. It exposes both the dominant culture of a given context and those others that simultaneously help to authorize it. In this way, history becomes plural, contested and various. It is comprised of moments that are both similar to each other *and* markedly different. Such a perspective demands a more complex negotiation through the kinds of tensions and upheavals that marked medieval culture and society. It has an effect upon the kinds of readings of Chaucer we produce in the twenty-first century.

In the late 1980s, emphasis shifted from an understanding of Chaucer as an orthodox Christian exegete, or else as an ironic humanist (see E. Talbot Donaldson). Instead he began to be regarded as a pluralistic author, one actively and deliberately avoiding single solutions. Many now grasp Chaucer as 'postmodern', an idea generated, in part, through his use of conflicting voices, styles and genres. By 'postmodern', I mean to suggest that he rejects moral truths and certainties in favour of ambiguities. Also, that he turns attention away from central forces of power like Church and government, to examine, instead, the margins and contestations of that power. There are many ways in which critics might engage these issues. One is to look more closely at voice and narration. Chaucer usually employs a narrator with a distinctive voice and apparently personal slant to relate his tales. He then allows the narrator to stand between himself, as an author, and what he actually writes. In the light of this, early critics emphasize Chaucer's irony. Later studies adapt this view to argue instead that narrators and 'their' texts are performative. They are not psychologically real, but a constructed, textual drama that stands outside real life. This drama works between text and audience and cuts across the different voices in a text. Others engage differently the problems of 'voice'.

H. Marshall Leicester investigates this issue via deconstruction, an approach that stresses the *text* and its workings out, rather than the author. At the same time, he offers a psychoanalytical reading to suggest that several of Chaucer's speakers (the Wife, the Pardoner, the Knight) create an apparently real social self. So, their portraits seem realistic but we are also constantly reminded that the text is, in fact, a fabrication. This gives rise to Leicester's famous suggestion of a 'disenchanted self' whereby what seems to be a real character or subject is instead a position, open to various and competing forces that all pass through and affect it. What we see in the *General Prologue* in particular is the effect of taken-for-granted, hidden factors upon a person: social power and its concealed nature, our unconscious desires, and covert structures of language. Chaucer deconstructs his world to expose it as an ideological construction constantly buffeted by other forces. Such a perspective takes us well away from the concept of literature as allegory, divinely ordained by an author-God. It insists that a text generates meanings outside and beyond the control or intent of its author.

Despite this, Leicester's work still manages to suggest that Chaucer occupies a special position as someone fully aware of the hidden forces noted earlier, yet, seemingly so unaffected by them he can reveal their workings to us. This impasse is confronted by those critics who maintain that texts and the figures in them exceed the consciously creative intent of the author to spring from particular historical moments. This means that they are subject to a range of competing forces and disclosures so that a text speaks from several perspectives *all at the same time*. This idea is loosely based on the theories of the Russian Mikhail Bakhtin. He observed how a strong institution like the medieval Church speaks as one voice to present a monologic (single) perspective on authority to which everyone must conform. In contrast a dialogic text – *The Canterbury Tales*, according to some – offers competing voices or viewpoints that work in dialogue with each other. According to Bakhtin, such voices speak against the grain of an authority like Church teachings to air dissent. They operate as carnival, a scurrilous and irreverent safety valve of opposition. Such texts are not fully subversive, however, for carnival is 'holiday', time out that always reverts to the status quo of the dominant discourse.

NEW HISTORICISM

Ideas like these intersect the field of New Historicism. In order to identify those competing voices in the first instance, we need an acute awareness of history as far from monologic or monolithic. We must access these competing discourses and look at how they are sourced. In other words, we must uncover how what is said or written becomes a practice that binds certain social and cultural sub-groups. Literary texts of all kinds, and reading/writing practices, thus combine with legal, medical, political, religious and educational documents to ensure that we begin to read Chaucer as a product of his time. We read to explore how texts, including non-literary ones, were produced, circulated and received, in both the fourteenth century and beyond. A poem like *The Canterbury Tales* can have no fixed meaning because it remains one small part of other discourses. Equally, our historicized reading of it can only ever be suggestive, a reconstruction of a range of meanings on offer to a particular audience at a given time and generated through the ideas, beliefs, status and concerns of a particular readership. For New Historicists, all texts are constructed through a process of careful selection and recorded in a chosen form. We can never read Chaucer as a realist, faithfully depicting life exactly as it was in his time. Instead, we must ask *why* he constructed his work in the ways he did. What influenced his decisions, including his omissions? What do these choices reveal?

The impact of New Historicism upon Chaucer criticism is inestimable (see New Chaucer Society website, Section 6 of Further Reading). It has produced two critics of particular note: Paul Strohm and Lee Patterson. Strohm insists that we revisit the nature of Chaucer's audience. He identifies his actual audience as an emerging group of people like the author; not courtly as we often think, but those loosely allied to the aristocracy and its power base, though not of the same class. Strohm suggests that Chaucer writes for this actual audience, and, also, an ideal one that is a literary construct emerging from his stories (the Canterbury pilgrimage). This ensures that the *Tales* is a social text, a response to a transitional space that occurs in the fourteenth century as the economy shifts away from feudalism. Of particular appeal is the suggestion that the voices are not to be reconciled and that tension or contradiction can be left in play. Yet Strohm's emphasis at the same time upon the pilgrimage as a promise of cohesion and community seems to stress a Chaucer who is, finally, always conciliatory.

Patterson also stresses social context but, above all, he engages Leicester's attempt (made from a different theoretical perspective) to mediate society and self. Patterson imagines an exchange between the two. So, what we might call human nature – seen in the psychological realism of figures in the *Tales* – can be taken as universal, at precisely the same time that we recognize it springs from a specific cultural context. He famously offers the Pardoner as an example of how society and self come together in a difficult, dialectic relationship. He is 'social' in that he is created as a composite, with ideas taken from literary and medieval religious culture. In this way, Chaucer shows how the Pardoner is framed by those contexts. Yet Chaucer also offers us a figure who tries to define himself as separate from those contexts; we see his eye for fashion and alliance with the Summoner, his 'compeer', in the *General Prologue* for example, and, later, his professed liking for wine and women.

Patterson argues that we are all part of a social world and its practices whose enterprises we take for granted, and, so, forget to interrogate what he terms its 'acting out'. Instead, we should 'think socially', remain aware of this and its effects on us, at the same time as we recall our individuality or specificity (Patterson 1991: 155). Further, he suggests that this is something relevant to us today as well as to readings of Chaucer, a manoeuvre taken up in contemporary criticism; Carolyn Dinshaw's *Getting Medieval* (1999) examines the persistence of some ideologies through both medieval texts and contemporary popular culture in, for example, Tarantino's film *Pulp Fiction* (1994).

The weakness of both Strohm's and Patterson's highly influential perspective on Chaucer Studies seems, in part, bound with some of the weaknesses of a New Historicist approach. Their reference to Chaucer-the-author or Chaucer-the-man leads us back to the conundrum of how to recover authorial intention. In particular, both offer Chaucer as a visionary, one able to see through the manoeuvres and 'acting-out' that is, by their definition, concealed from us, to critique his own time. Patterson also puts forward a notion of the 'universal human' or self, an idea seemingly at odds with a New Historicist emphasis upon the particular contingent circumstances through which everybody and everything is constructed and re-evaluated across time.

GENDER STUDIES

Readers of Chaucer's work return time and again to the contradictions and tensions which mark it. This provides fertile ground for many critical approaches. Marxist and feminist criticism frequently overlap, despite their disparate agendas. Both begin by asking similar questions of texts, even if they subsequently draw different conclusions. Each looks for gaps and silences, the 'not-said' of a text revealed by ambiguity, clashes, telling omissions and endings that either lack resolution or are unsatisfactory or impossible. It is, however, important to draw some distinction between the two fields.

A Marxist approach seeks to identify dominant ideologies at work in a text. These may be expressed directly through, for example, the Parson's sermon in the case of religion or more obliquely in the form of a satirical attack upon the practices of its officials. This is then set against an analysis of uneasy or ambivalent moments where ideology is called into question, and not necessarily by the author. So, David Aers reads the *Clerk's Tale* through an examination of how power, represented by Walter, operates. He suggests it depends on the acquiescence of others, like obedient Griselda who must swear an oath of allegiance to her husband. Aers links this to the unstable politics of England in the 1390s with its challenge to the idea of absolute submission (exemplified by the monarchy in real life and by Walter in the tale), seen when Griselda subtly questions Walter's authority. Aers admits that Chaucer can never be the 'Mr Average' of the Middle Ages, then proceeds to offer him as such, in some of his early critical writing at least. He does suggest that Chaucer critiques those overarching frameworks of his own time: the Church, politics and power, authority, gender, chivalry.

I implied earlier that the notion of selfhood is as inflected a category as any other 'historical' reconstruction. This issue is taken up by both psychoanalytical readings and feminist/gender studies to impact upon Chaucer criticism in a huge way. A feminist literary enterprise is concerned with the ways in which a gender identity that does not simply correlate to biological sex is constructed. It focuses moreover upon the dynamics of gender, sexuality and power.

The impact of Carolyn Dinshaw and Elaine Tuttle Hansen on questions of gender in Chaucer is inestimable. Dinshaw's *Chaucer Sexual Poetics* (1989) was the first book-length feminist work on Chaucer. It celebrates a feminine it defines as a socially constructed and problematic category, rather than simply exploring from the standpoint of the 'woman' in the text. Dinshaw's starting point, one shared by many feminists, is that certain activities are explicitly gendered, or else somehow crucial to our understanding of how relations between genders become embedded and 'natural'. So, the medieval notion of *auctoritas* is not masculine just because only men tend to have access to it, but because it connotes ideas designated *as* masculine – definitive answers or explanations offered as authority. For Dinshaw, one of these practices is reading and the ways in which ideals and issues cut across texts. To read like a man (not necessarily *as* a man) is to strip the surface text (described as a captive woman's body) and penetrate it to reveal its allegorical meaning. To read like a woman is, in contrast, to interpret only literally.

Dinshaw's more recent work is more broadly located in a gender studies that owes much to Hansen's seminal feminist volume, *Chaucer and the Fictions of Gender* (1992). Hansen also explores medieval practices of reading and writing and their impact upon Chaucer's texts. Where Dinshaw is radical though, Hansen offers only a cautious endorsement of Chaucer as a feminist writer. Instead, she concludes that his apparent interest in this area reveals anxieties about masculinity and its construction, rather than femininity. Her initial search for a genuinely feminine voice yields only silences and gaps. She suggests that Chaucer's texts are symptomatic of his culture and its ideologies, rather than an escape from or subversion of it.

Hansen's work paved the way for a Masculinity Studies that remains integral to feminist criticism. One of the most obvious examples of its concerns is witnessed in a reading of the *Knight's Tale* along the lines of my own discussion in Chapter 3. Both Feminisms and Maculinities increasingly locate within the broader field of Gender Studies. It is easy to gauge the impact of theorists like Judith Butler upon this area (see Chapter 4). Butler (1990) insists that gender does not exist as an easily defined category. Nor is it a tailor-made attribute we can choose, let alone something that is determined by biology. Instead, it is culturally and socially constructed via a process that is continuous and endlessly repeated. The effect of this repetition is to render it 'natural' and to disguise the fact that gender is performative. By this, I mean that we act out over and again what we think gender means in our culture. In so doing, we add to the illusion that it is a stable and discrete category.

This idea of gender as always negotiated and repeatedly performed ensures that it is always in danger of slipping out of what we think defines and bounds it, most notably that 'masculine' is set up as dominant over its opposite 'feminine' (remember that neither of these categories necessarily relate to sex, but instead refer to a range of characteristics and strategies that we associate with each). Queer theory is especially attracted by moments in texts that unsettle a masculine–feminine binary. Again, the thinking is that such instances work to expose as false our conviction that gender – and its concomitants like sexuality and power – is secure. Its agenda is not necessarily to expose a text, a character or an author as 'gay'. Rather, 'to queer' a text is to 'queer-y' it, to open it up for interrogation and to read against the grain of apparently normative heterosexual ideals. Queer readings might be generated in numerous ways: through exploration of gaps, tensions, or moments that, however implicitly, might suggest same-sex desire; through erotic or sexually resonant language; through mirroring or correspondences in terms of behaviours, speech, vocabulary or repeated motifs and images; and through 'touches', both literal or implied. The 'touch of the queer' is famously proposed in an article by Carolyn Dinshaw (1995). There she opens an elaboration of her thinking through consideration of the disturbing visual image of the supermodel Cindy Crawford's hand upon the arm of the androgynous singer k.d. lang as she prepares to shave her face.

Much queer debate in Chaucer Studies circles around the figure of the Pardoner. Kruger reclaims the Pardoner for a gay history that pre-dates our modern definition of homosexual (see Chapter 4). He celebrates what he perceives as the Pardoner's disruption of the dominant heterosexuality of medieval culture. Kruger insists that we read against the probable homophobic intentions of the author (and certainly against those of his audiences) and the likely moral condemnation of a character like the Pardoner in Chaucer's time. Such a reading rightly spotlights the difficulties inherent in any interpretation of a figure whose gender is offered as simultaneously ambiguous and significant. Equally, of course, a text may well exceed that largely illegible notion of authorial intention. Though Kruger's historicism elsewhere in his article is richly applied, he seems to understand 'queer' as simply 'homosexual'. This slips the Pardoner right out of his medieval context into a contemporary and a narrower debate about gays.

Others offer a more skilful negotiation of some of the difficulties raised by Kruger's singular queer interpretation.

Dinshaw (1995) presents a nuanced reading of the Pardoner's anomalous body, as well as a clear outline of the kinds of connections we might seek when turning a queer lens onto Chaucer's work. Glenn Burger and Karma Lochrie (see Further Reading) demonstrate the overlap between queer and gender theory when examining the *Miller's Tale*. Lochrie (1994) neatly side steps the charge of imposition that Kruger fails by carefully contextualizing her views. She argues that though the *Miller's Tale* problematizes gender and sexuality, it does so through a specifically medieval understanding of adultery and cuckoldry. Here, both are linked to the male-to-male transmission of jokes, secrets and knowledge about women. So, the open secret of cuckoldry is that one man takes advantage of another by making love to his wife. As a result, the tale centres on male rivalry and, thus, how both masculinity and femininity are made to mean.

More recent strands of Chaucer criticism include eco or green readings and postcolonial theories. To some extent, these are in the process of development and, as such, perhaps side step as yet some of the objections to which other fields remain susceptible. Like feminist and Marxist approaches, postcolonial critics search for gaps and suppressions to re-vision texts and allow subdued voices to have their say. In particular, these voices or moments in a text allow us to revisit the ways in which Chaucer (as a nationalistic poet) and his contribution to literature as the 'Father of English poetry' have a hand in narrating stories of our origins, or how nations and nationalities are negotiated and constructed.

Such readings, in common with others, take us ever further from that early Chaucer Studies with its emphasis on scholarly research, editing practices and manuscript or material evidence. They move away from a discrete 'history' and from Christian, allegorical readings, divided from, and somehow prior to, contemporary concerns. Rather, those engaged in criticism today, whatever their field, seek active links between past, present and back again. They speculate on what their theories and our time have in common with each other, and also with a medieval culture that is, nevertheless, recognized as specific and particular.

RESEARCH SUGGESTIONS

1. Investigate any 'field' of your choice with the following questions in mind: What are its strengths and limitations? What is its place within a wider critical web? Does it enhance that web or offer a fresh perspective on texts or previous critical readings?
2. Should contemporary theoretical ideas and practices be applied to medieval texts and/or those works subsequently read divorced from their medieval context?

CHAPTER 5

AFTERLIVES

Extant in our archives is the famous Ellesmere manuscript of Chaucer's *Tales*. Its design is lavish and its cost clearly exorbitant. Whoever commissioned it greatly esteemed Chaucer's work. What a manuscript like this suggests to us is something of the ways in which Chaucer's reputation evolves. The state of his texts, as Carolyn Collette puts it, is directly allied to that of his reputation. Both are subject to interpretation, as evidenced by the manuscripts that are left to us, 'each of which acts like a unique set of binoculars, adjusted to somebody else's eyesight' (Collette 2002: 20).

Chaucer's work initially circulated in manuscript form as miscellany, or loosely organized anthology. By the sixteenth century, his poems began to appear as printed folio editions, versions of our contemporary books. This is the form in which they remained until well into the 1700s. Why should we examine the composition of these manuscripts and folio collections? In the first place, they tell us something about the material production of texts. But this becomes especially important once we realize that it reveals something about how Chaucer's work was received into the nexus of commentary and interpretation I remarked on in Chapters 1 and 2. At the heart of this reception is paradox. As we have seen, medieval notions of authorship de-emphasize authorial control and intent in favour of audience and reading. Yet Chaucer's reputation, perhaps uniquely, is oddly situated. Though his reputation has varied through the centuries, it seems always to have been bound by an 'understanding' of him as an actual person. Yet the 'facts' of Chaucer's life were obscured until relatively recently. A silence like that is an open invitation for compilers and critics alike to project their own notions and construct a 'Chaucer' to fit their time and tastes.

When an editor gathers Chaucer's work into a folio, he makes a series of choices and, so, substantially influences the final product. His selection is based on both commercial acumen and critical judgement. Editors and compilers put together a range of work chosen on the basis of social and literary tastes (which change over time) and package it in a way that suggests the scope of Chaucer's influence. They produce a Chaucer text according to what *they* think is important, and decide on the order of the material. Usually those earlier sixteenth-century folio editions reproduced the collections gathered up in manuscript form during, and immediately after, Chaucer's lifetime. But the folio compilers also recognized that 'Chaucer' was a brand that sells. As one of the few named authors working in the vernacular, to begin with at least, Chaucer's name was a marketable commodity. Its commercial value seems such that it shifted 'books' in a way multiple-authored collections, or even anonymous ones, did not.

One of the more unusual results of these ideas is the inclusion in folio editions of works spuriously attributed to Chaucer. We know now that these texts were authored by others. Some were anonymous, but many we recognize: Lydgate's *Siege of Thebes*, for example, was often placed alongside Chaucer's *Knight's Tale* where it functions as a prologue or opening section, and for years the medieval Scots writer Robert Henryson's *Testament of Cresseid* was believed to be the final book of Chaucer's *Troilus and Criseyde*. These tales – often called *apocrypha* or the apocryphal canon – remain crucial to any discussion of Chaucer's early reception, not least because he is the only English writer substantially affected by their inclusion. Chaucer has some 84 spurious tales; Shakespeare's false attribution is in single figures. Why do the folio compilers make these claims?

It may well be that because medieval notions of 'author' were slippery, the significance of the name 'Chaucer' was equally ambiguous; not so much unimportant as *open*. Since medieval texts were unstable and collaborative in enterprise, carelessness, or even lack of concern, over authorial inscription was probably commonplace. The question of authenticity was largely irrelevant in a world that valued *memoria* and *auctoritas*, rather than originality. At the same time, an emerging print culture ensures that texts begin to circulate differently and for wider, more varied audiences. 'Book' circulates as a material object but lacks discrete definition, for its basis is still manuscript anthology, that collection of all kinds of material without a single focus.

Therefore, to ascribe a folio or 'book' to Chaucer recalls a range of often competing manoeuvres. To sign the name 'Chaucer' is a commercial strategy in which works genuinely by Chaucer sit alongside others which are falsely attributed to him to offer a book that is 'Chaucerian' in flavour or style, rather than authentic. Some spurious attribution may well have been genuine error. But it is equally possible that some editors knew the work was not actually Chaucer's, perhaps choosing to include spurious works in order to give value for money. Certainly, some folios include a standard get-out clause in the title, citing 'Chaucer' and the more ambiguous phrase 'diverse works never in print before' (Thynne).

For at least the first 100 years after his death, and beyond, Chaucer's work was continuously in print regardless of its authenticity. This disputed, apocryphal Chaucerian canon was not finally stabilized until the late nineteenth century. What, if anything, is the value of looking at texts we now know for certain were never written by Chaucer? Some of the apocryphal stories falsely attributed to Chaucer in the past reveal much about the afterlife of *The Canterbury Tales*. Equally, they tell us something about Chaucer's literary reception: about him as a writer, as well as the reading tastes and practices of successive generations of audiences. The sheer number of these stories testifies to Chaucer's continuing influence on other writers. Many are inspired by a need to 'write back' to or engage with Chaucer's narratives, a process aided by the incomplete state of the *Tales* and a partial or receding dramatic frame that implicitly invites others to fill in the gaps. Some collections offer a version of the *Plowman's Tale* which for many years was thought to be the 'missing' story of the Plowman who appears in Chaucer's *General Prologue* but never tells a tale. Similarly, what we now recognize as Lydgate's *Siege of Thebes* may have been attributed to Chaucer because it reads as a lengthy prologue to the *Knight's Tale*. Elsewhere some pilgrims allegedly recount second tales; the Merchant apparently tells the *Prologue and the Tale of Beryn*, for example. Yet in *The Canterbury Tales* none does, even though to speak twice is part of Harry Bailly's challenge.

More importantly, the spurious attributions are an integral feature of a hermeneutic web in which to read and write is to contribute to and contest meaning. In the *Tale of Beryn*, the Merchant purports to relate how one of his fellows in the dramatic frame, the Pardoner, unsuccessfully tries to seduce a barmaid. Its impetus seems to be taken from the Pardoner's own boastful self-display in Chaucer's *Pardoner's Prologue* that he has a pretty wench in every town or inn that he frequents. The anonymous author of *Beryn* picks up on this detail and adds it to the Pardoner's later suggestion to the Wife of Bath that he was once going to marry. In so doing he places the figure of the Pardoner in a heterosexual frame that problematizes further discussion of what many critics perceive to be his ambiguous sexuality, and so re-ignites academic debate about how the Pardoner 'means'.

Similarly, the critical reception of Chaucer's *Troilus and Criseyde* was affected greatly by the addition in many printed collections of Chaucer of what we now realize is Robert Henryson's *Testament of Cresseid*. For many years this was widely accepted as the sixth and final book of Chaucer's five-book poem. As such, it takes us well away from the ambivalences of Chaucer's version, especially its open and unsatisfactory ending. Henryson's 'addition' offers a moral resolution missing in Chaucer in the form of a resounding criticism of Criseyde's sexual treachery; she is punished by contracting leprosy and left contrite but so disfigured that Troilus no longer recognizes her. This is a working out that remains at odds with Chaucer's narrator's anxious and ambivalent attitude towards the question of her loyalty. Such foreclosure is also opposed to contemporary critical engagement with Chaucer's *Troilus and Criseyde* and the range of reactions it sparks. Yet Henryson begins his version by asking not if Criseyde is true, but if all that Chaucer *wrote* is true. By shifting attention to the narration and the processes of story-telling, he questions the nature of authority, an issue which is the hallmark of Chaucer's own work. In other words, Henryson writes back to Chaucer in a way that can also open up our own readings of Chaucer. These spurious pieces may, then, be active responses to questions, ambiguities and tensions in Chaucer's work. They participate in the nexus of commentary and 'glosynge' so familiar to medieval culture and engage a process of reading or interpretation and critical debate at the heart of our own world. In this way, Chaucer's works continue to circulate and stay alive, however different from their first appearance in print.

INFLUENCING OTHERS

Part of this afterlife is Chaucer's extensive influence on other writers. I do not intend to offer an exhaustive study here but, instead, to note both its considerable extent and the diversity of his appeal: from Dryden and Pope, through to the Romantic poets and John Masefield, on to William Morris, short story writers like Jack London and Rudyard Kipling, and up to James Joyce, W. B. Yeats, Scott Fitzgerald, Margaret Atwood, Caryl Churchill and Alice Walker. Just as the folio compilers of the sixteenth century packaged a commodity called 'Chaucer' and privileged a particular understanding or version of his works, so, too, this disparate list of authors read Chaucer in a variety of ways.

Masefield visualizes Chaucer as part of an image of a timeless, rural England. A pastoral 'Chaucer' similarly influences Keats and Shelley who appreciate this version of the author for his elegies and courtly love poems as well as the spurious *The Flower and the Leaf* and *The Cuckoo and the Nightingale*. The art and narrative poetry of William Morris is heavily imbued with a sense of Chaucer as a classical and formal writer, a love poet above all else. His is a typically nineteenth-century pre-Raphaelite Chaucer, a romantic writer of nature and dream-visions. Morris's Kelmscott Press gives us a famous edition of *The Canterbury Tales* illustrated by Edward Burne-Jones. The Kelmscott volume (1896) is renowned for its luxurious paper, its elaborate art work and intricately decorated margins. It is an eye-catching 'Chaucer' whose impetus is deliberately nostalgic. Morris's own interest in art prompts an attempt to evoke an idea of the medieval book or manuscript before the advent of mass printing, even though, in many respects, Morris's 'Chaucer' is out of step with Victorian thinking on the man and his works.

One of the major themes of the late Victorian 'Chaucer' influenced popular reception right up to World War II. In this tradition, Chaucer is presented as an embodiment of 'Englishness'. The focus is usually upon the *Tales*, to the exclusion of all other works, as a poem expressing nationalistic sentiment. Just as earlier, Dryden called him the 'Father of English Poetry' (1700), so too G. K. Chesterton praises Chaucer for being the 'Father of his Country' (1932). This is a paternalistic view of Chaucer as a genial, humorous fellow speaking in the vernacular (English) for a 'merrie Englande'. Within this frame, Chaucer is seen as the epitome of ordinariness and representative of values like charity, fellowship and fraternity. In part, this view springs from the medieval Ellesmere manuscript portrait of Chaucer as a portly man-of-the-world. It is aggravated by conflating (an imagined) Chaucer-the-author with the fictional role of Chaucer-the-pilgrim in the *Tales*: Chaucer 'becomes' a bumbling, self-effacing and down-to-earth figure who appeals to a common humanity thought to exist somewhere in idyllic England. This is the Chaucer perpetrated by a large number of US writers who seemingly buy into a tourist package based on such ideals, one divorced from historical actualities and reminiscent of our own contemporary popular culture, which persists with a tendency to categorize Chaucer as irreverent and bawdy, obsessed with sexual shenanigans and breaking wind.

Other more seriously theoretical 'Chaucers' co-exist, seemingly without conflict. James Joyce extrapolates for his own writings a postmodern Chaucer composed of numerous competing narrative voices, as well as connecting with the problematics of Chaucer's tales, especially their endings, or lack of them. Atwood, Churchill, Walker, and Scott Fitzgerald also engage these issues. Early on in literary history, Pope's interest in women and the presentation of the feminine extended to a translation of the *Wife of Bath's Prologue*. This presages a contemporary intersection with feminist or gender theory and issues seen in several women writers, an intervention that fuels the continued debate over whether Chaucer is generally sympathetic to women or a traditional anti-feminist. Caryl Churchill's *Top Girls* (1982), Alice Walker's *The Color Purple* (1983) and Margaret Atwood's *The Handmaid's Tale* (1987) are all loosely based on or refer to Chaucer's tale of patient Griselda suffering under patriarchal tyranny in the *Clerk's Tale*. At the same time, each of these writers confronts and attempts to turn around a masculine textual appropriation of an emerging feminine voice. This is an issue Chaucer begins to explore through the alternative readings invoked in the 'Song of the Envoy' at the end of the *Clerk's Tale*. There, its call for women to speak up and out against anti-feminist edicts in keeping with the Wife of Bath's mode of defence, directly contradicts the Clerk's 'inportable' [impossible] but exemplary ideal of stoic women (VII, 1163–212). Its continued contemporary relevance is witnessed in the unusual narrative techniques employed by those women writers who retell, however obliquely, Griselda's story some 600 years later. Churchill repeatedly allows her historical female figures of Act I to speak simultaneously, both to echo and to drown out each other's words. Alice Walker's novel uses first-person narration and recollection, often in the form of diaries and letters. A first-person account in *The Handmaid's Tale* is ruptured by the reductive lecture-style 'Notes' at its end. Here, Atwood refuses to permit the feminine voice she has constructed to be wiped out by a masculine academic discourse that seeks to deny its authenticity.

Chaucer's continued presence in popular culture also merits attention. Versions of his work reappear in children's literature, especially during the Edwardian period, and testify both to the power of his narratives and, perhaps, to an understanding of him as an author who offers moral instruction. P. C. Doherty's medieval murder mysteries book series (1994) is partially constructed around the notion of Chaucer's pilgrims telling new tales. Our fascination with whom or what Chaucer was is seemingly reflected in his occasional appearances as 'Chaucer' elsewhere, none of which cohere into a definitive or singular 'authentic' man. Anya Seton's *Katherine* (1954) includes portraits of Chaucer and his wife who are attached to the influential household of John of

Gaunt through the relationship between his wife and her sister Katherine (Gaunt's mistress and, eventually, third wife). Perhaps less well known are Emily Riching's *In Chaucer's Maytime* (1902), a sentimental examination of Chaucer's courtship of his wife, Philippa, and their married life together, and *Deputy for Youth*, where Wallace Nichols (1935) has some discussion of the Cecily de Chaumpaigne rape case.

BEYOND PRINT?

More recently 'Chaucer' plays a part in Brian Helgeland's *A Knight's Tale* (2001). The film owes much to a Chaucer it imagines as a free-wheeling, radical figure interested in ambiguities of gender. These are played out within an inversion of the traditional romance structure where the good guy still gets the heroine but, improbably, escapes his peasant status to become noble by virtue of merit, not birth. Its plot is only loosely that of Chaucer's *Knight's Tale* with its focus on masculine rivalry and aggression and its 'official' outlet, the medieval tournament. It includes feisty women (the Lady and a female blacksmith whose armour is superior to any men might make), camp moments, and a 'gay' soundtrack, plus long, lingering glances between male characters and slow-motion shots of phallic lances trying to penetrate armour.

Chaucer's poems also reappear as film, musical, television and radio adaptations. There are BBC radio versions of the *Tales* (1946 and 1991) and TV showings of it in 1969, 1998–2000 and 2003. In the BBC1 1998 adaptation, the stories were animated which allowed for an interesting visual interpretation. Six tales occupied each half-hour slot and were transmitted twice, once in Middle English verse and again in modern prose. Though this greatly abridged the work, the translation broadened its appeal. This was further aided by setting humour alongside darker, more sinister motifs such as death, violence and plague. Such a reading is a refreshing alternative to previous popular versions of Chaucer which, going for the broadest, most immediate appeal, once again, tend to stress Chaucer and his *Tales* as a personification of 'merrie Englande' composed of fellowship, *fabliaux* and plenty of ale.

Nevertheless, these interventions in popular culture do provide an opportunity for widening Chaucer's audience and keep him in the public forum. Adaptations of his work also seem entirely in keeping with a medieval literary enterprise which, as we have seen throughout this book, adhere to no notion of authorial control or copyright regulations, and continually recycle stories within a narrative dynamic that includes readers' commentaries and reactions. For Chaucer's verse to shift to the genre of drama seems equally fitting. Chaucer had an abiding interest in confounding our expectations regarding generic conventions and structures while the oral, more performative qualities of the *Tales* composed entirely of narrative voices is especially suited to radio, TV and theatrical performance. For example, casting Alison as a successful television performer in the BBC's 2003 adaptation of the Wife of Bath's story, foregrounds precisely these qualities. The piece also uses the camera as a confessional device that both spotlights the Wife's love of performance and drama, and allows her to talk directly, in monologue, to an invisible viewing audience.

With this in mind some reactions to the BBC's 2003 screening of six of the *Canterbury Tales* appear incomprehensible. Accusations from within both academia and the broad sheet press of 'dumbing-down' or of losing the 'essence' of an 'original', which as we have seen can never be discovered, elide the provocations of a series that offers not translated or modernized renditions of Chaucer but *new* versions, where the *Tales* is only a starting point for ideas. As such, some adhere more closely to their chosen story than others. Regardless, all engage these narratives in ways pertinent to our contemporary world, and, at times, to the contemporary face of critical studies on Chaucer. The *Sea-Captain's (Shipman's) Tale* is set in London's Asian business community and, like its namesake, centres on sex, fraternal ties and money. The *Pardoner's Tale* is violent and uncompromising with three low-life lads helping out in a search for a missing teenage girl. In a gesture to postcolonialism, the *Man of Law's Tale* recounts the story of a young Nigerian refugee found in a boat near Chatham and the effects of her arrival on those around her.

The first pair of tales in the series – the *Miller's Tale* and the *Wife of Bath's Tale* (or, rather, her *Prologue*) – offer particularly interesting readings of Chaucer's two Alisons. Contrary to what we might expect, the women are presented as victims with little control over their own destiny. The Alison of the *Miller's Tale* is, like the men, thoroughly duped by the stranger and con-man figure representing Nicholas. We last see her standing on the roadside waiting for him to keep his promise to take her away and make her a star. In the *Wife's Tale*, an acclaimed but ageing TV star takes up with her young co-actor when her husband leaves her for another woman. The young man assaults and abandons her, and then briefly returns before disappearing again to leave her alone, talking to the camera of love, as she does at the start.

For me, the most innovative of these six renderings was the *Knight's Tale*. Here, two old friends meet up again in prison where they sign up for an English class. Both fall in love with their teacher who clearly returns the feelings of the Palamon character. When 'Arcite' is released on licence, his friend, torn apart by a jealous conviction that he will seek out their teacher, escapes from prison to confront them. The ending is a powerful and terrifying one with 'Arcite' setting fire to himself once he realizes the homo-erotic bond he shares with his friend – and which has been intimated throughout – has been ruptured. But what is exceptional is the way in which the *Knight's Tale's* themes of violence, surveillance and control manifest through CCTV cameras, cell-door spyholes, keys, compulsory searches and locked gates. At the same time, the crushing force of the state, represented by Theseus in Chaucer, is re-read through social workers, police, prison warders, the prison governor and those legal and educational institutions that, as in Chaucer's version, seem to unleash chaos rather than secure order.

Described in the advertising blurb as a 'new adaptation', the Royal Shakespeare Company performed *The Canterbury Tales* in two parts in autumn 2005 at the Swan Theatre, Stratford-upon-Avon, taking the performances on a national UK tour in 2006. Mike Poulton wrote the text in a largely faithful rendering of Middle English, described on the RSC's website as retaining the 'flavour of the original' to keep, for example, Chaucer's ten-syllable line and rhyming couplets (see Further Reading).

The plays were directed by Gregory Doran, and two associate directors, Rebecca Gatwood and Jonathan Munby in, I think, a spirit of collaboration akin to medieval 'text' production. Each has their own style and set of techniques so that *Sir Thopas* is delivered as a rap, the *Manciple's Tale* as a mini-opera and the *Nun's Priest's* as a puppet show. Where Rebecca Gatwood 'wanted to wave the flag for some of the women in Chaucer', Jonathan Munby liked poems like the *Prioress's Tale* 'that provoked me the most . . . asking me to question something.' All of the directors agreed, though, that though they would keep, in the main, the traditional order of the tales, they would edit and cut some of them (there is no *Canon's Yeoman's Tale*); even so, Part I ran for over two and a half hours, and Part II for more than two. Equally, all those working on the productions saw Chaucer's work as 'dramatic narrative poems to be spoken'. In order to enhance this aspect, rehearsals consisted of reading aloud to begin with and then followed a constant process of alteration to reach 'the heart of the drama'.

I can only applaud this long-overdue enterprise for its emphasis upon collaboration, performance, language and process. I end, however, on a note of puzzlement, in which Chaucer's conflicted place in matters of nationhood and 'Englishness' once again comes to the fore. The RSC's *Canterbury Tales* website continually compares Chaucer to our current national hero, Shakespeare, to find the former wanting. It describes the *Tales* as 'rich source material for Shakespeare' and comments that Chaucer reflects 'every facet of human nature, as did Shakespeare'. Apparently, 'all of Shakespeare's plays [are] reflected directly or indirectly' in *The Canterbury Tales*; the *Man of Law's Tale*, for instance, is dismissed as a 20-minute *Pericles*. It seems that writers are still co-opted for nationalistic means and in order to establish a stable, linear and progressive literary heritage, each sourcing and inspiring the work of those who come later. Perhaps we should expect no more than this reduction: this is, after all, the Royal Shakespeare Company, with a vested interest in promoting that particular author. It seems a pity that just when Chaucer's incursion into a contemporary popular afterlife begins to feel a little more assured, it slips to fall back as a mere quirk of history.

We continue to remain fascinated by Chaucer-the-man and his work. But to conclude that this is because his work has universal appeal and speaks to us across generations is both glib and misses the point. Instead, I suggest any survey reveals the conflicted nature of a text's afterlife, the constructed nature of a 'Chaucer' we interpret differently and variously. Which is he: genial Everyman and humorous representative of 'merrie Englande'; inspiration for other 'greats'; anti-clerical satirist and subverter of authority; worldly diplomatic man of the court, nationalistic or love poet? Chaucer is, of course, all of these at once, caught in a network of pluralities, contradictions and ambiguities that, as we have seen, orient the *Tales* itself.

HERE AND NOW

One final incursion into popular culture deserves special mention. Once confined only to the academy, to education, scholarship and examination syllabi in schools and universities, Chaucer Studies has spilled onto the internet. It is, admittedly, a small step, little removed from the connected institutions of academia and publishing that frequently spawn the websites and electronic resources devoted to his work. Two aspects give me cause for optimism, though. The internet, with its ease of access and widespread availability, has the potential to bring a new, larger audience to Chaucer, especially in connection with projects such as the recent BBC1 adaptations or, perhaps, as part of the writing initiatives of the kind the BBC promoted alongside the screenings. Here, an open competition invited young adults, many with little knowledge of Chaucer, to script their own version of a tale, the winning entry to be read on Radio 4. Equally, when commissioning the series scripts were taken from three established writers, plus three without a previous publication record.

Second, translations of Chaucer's texts, most of them electronic, are paradoxically evidence of both an increasing popularity and/or the way in which he has slipped out of our mainstream culture. In part, a perceived difficulty over understanding Middle English ensures that few will read in that language unless compelled by examination pressures. There is no doubt that medieval

English, with no standard dialect or established conventions of spelling and punctuation, presents the modern reader with problems. There are, however, many aids to negotiating this. Some electronic versions of the text offer a split-screen facility, original alongside modern verse. Others have audio clips and/or easily retrievable glossaries. In 1946, Neville Coghill translated the *Tales* for BBC radio, a rendition subsequently published by Penguin and still in print today.

The issue of translation is, in my view, compounded by the attitude of the Chaucer academy. There is a strong resistance to reading in anything other than Middle English from many leading scholars and critics who seem to fear that translations will replace that original and further narrow Chaucer's audience. School and college examination questions laudably promote close textual readings. In practice, this often leads to pedagogical emphasis on line by line translation – as with a foreign language text – and poetic technique to foreclose a more open or theoretical approach. Without wishing to gloss the apparent inaccessibility of Chaucer's language, over-emphasis upon it ensures we are in danger of relegating Chaucer to an irretrievable, historical past.

A good translation is a renewal. It will genuinely engage with language and versification, as well as critical issues, for there are many fine judgements to be made when selecting words or pieces of text and expressing their sense in contemporary idiom. The best are not replacements for the original Middle English, or simply modernizations. They reinvigorate texts and keep them alive, produce new versions of a story rather than a literal rendering of its source material. As Steve Ellis notes in his *Chaucer at Large* (Ellis 2000: 165) they are part of the nexus of commentary and exegesis of a source text, as much a writing-back as those spurious pieces I discussed earlier. Not everyone has an academic interest in Chaucer. Many of us benefit from having a framework upon which to hang plot and characterization before a detailed reading. As such we should use translation in a critical and aware manner. In so doing, we allow a new audience access to Chaucer's work, the most inspired or committed of whom may well go on to read in Chaucer's language.

REVIEW

An overview of the afterlife of Chaucer's works might tell us something

- of changing literary tastes and practices of reading and writing
- of the political manoeuvres and social issues, a context that alters over time, that we bring to bear on the texts we interpret, as well as those we author
- of the difficulty of ever recovering an authentic author-God called 'Chaucer' or of establishing an original, definitive text of *The Canterbury Tales*.

To discuss notions of authorial intention in connection with Chaucer is, as I have suggested throughout, at best problematic, and at worst anathema. Further, it seems increasingly irrelevant to seek an authoritative concept of Chaucer and/or his works when these same texts display a vigorous interrogation of *auctoritas* in all its manifestations. As a result, we are left with a continual re-branding or packaging of 'Chaucer' across the centuries, none of which is privileged and all of which contribute in their own ways to a complex understanding of his place in cultural history.

DISCUSSION QUESTIONS

1. Should we read Chaucer's works only in Middle English? Are we in danger of devaluing his work if we do not?
2. What notion of 'Chaucer' did you bring to your reading of the *Tales?* Has your perspective altered at all?
3. What do you understand by the notion of authenticity in connection with Chaucer? In your opinion, should adaptations of Chaucer's work be authentic?

FURTHER READING

1. CONTEXTS

Brewer, D. S. (1998), *A New Introduction to Chaucer*, 2nd edition. London and New York: Longman.

Cannon, Christopher (1993), '*Raptus* in the Chaumpaigne release and a newly discovered document concerning the life of Geoffrey Chaucer', in *Speculum*, 68, 74–94.

Dillon, Janette (1993), *Geoffrey Chaucer*. Basingstoke: Macmillan. This readable account of Chaucer's works has chapters on his life and on the medieval context in which he wrote.

Dyer, Christopher (2002), *Making a Living in the Middle Ages: the People of Britian, 850–1520*. New Haven, CT: Yale University Press. This gives a thorough account of the medieval economy and its effects on society.

Ellis, Steve (1996), *Geoffrey Chaucer, Writers and their Work*. Plymouth: Northcote House. This is a short, engaging study of Chaucer's works with a brief outline of his life story.

Ellis, Steve (ed.) (2005), *Chaucer: An Oxford Guide*. Oxford: Oxford University Press, 7–252. See Part I of this volume for a good selection of essays on medieval culture and the historical context of Chaucer's work.

Evans, Ruth (2005), 'Chaucer's Life', in Ellis (ed.), *Chaucer: An Oxford Guide*, 9–25.

Jones, Terry, Robert Yeager, Terry Dolan, Alan Fletcher and Juliette Dor (2002), *Who Murdered Chaucer? A Medieval Mystery*. London: Methuen.

Machan, Tim (2002), 'Texts', in Peter Brown (ed.), *A Companion To Chaucer*. Oxford: Blackwell, 428–42.

Pearsall, Derek (1992), *The Life of Geoffrey Chaucer: A Critical Biography*. Oxford: Blackwell. This is probably the best and most authoritative account of Chaucer's life.

Rhodes, Jim (2005), 'Religion', in Ellis (ed.), *Chaucer: An Oxford Guide* , 81–96.

Rigby, Steve (1996), *Chaucer in Context: Society, Allegory and Gender*. Manchester: Manchester University Press. Written in a clear and informed style, this volume seeks to place Chaucer's work in its historical context and explores the conflicting results of this search. It also has an excellent, general bibliography.

—— (2003), *A Companion to Britain in the Later Middle Ages*. Oxford: Blackwell. This comprehensive book has chapters on all aspects of medieval society and culture, plus a further reading section.

2. LANGUAGE, STYLE AND FORM

Burnley, David (2002), 'Language', in Brown (ed.), *A Companion to Chaucer*, 235–50.

Cannon, Christopher (1998), *The Making of Chaucer's English: A Study of Words*. Cambridge: Cambridge University Press.

Correale, Robert M. and Mary Hamel (eds) (2002), *Sources and Analogues of the 'Canterbury Tales'*, in *Chaucer Studies*. Woodbridge: Brewer.

Eckhardt, Caroline (2002), 'Genre', in Brown (ed.), *A Companion to Chaucer*, 180–94.

Horobin, Simon (2003), *The Language of the Chaucer Tradition*. Cambridge: Brewer. This looks at manuscript evidence, at the way scribes and editors transmitted Chaucer's work immediately after his death, and also tries to reconstruct Chaucer's language.

Lehrer, Seth (1996), *Reading from the Margins: Textual Studies, Chaucer and Medieval Literature*. San Marino: The Huntington Library.

Minkova, Donka (2005), 'Chaucer's language: pronunciation, morphology, metre', in Ellis (ed.), *Chaucer: An Oxford Guide*, 130–57.

Plummer, John F. (2002), 'Style', in Brown (ed.), *A Companion to Chaucer*, 414–27.

Wogan-Browne, Jocelyn, Nicholas Watson, Andrew Taylor and Ruth Evans (eds) (1999), *The Idea of the Vernacular: An Anthology of Middle English Literary Theory, 1280–1520*. Exeter: University of Exeter Press. This is an interesting collection of writings about English, authorship and medieval readers/audiences.

3. READING *THE CANTERBURY TALES*

Beidler, Peter (ed.) (1998), *Masculinities in Chaucer*. Cambridge: D. S. Brewer.

Burger, Glenn (2000), 'Erotic discipline . . . or "Tee hee, I like my boys to be girls": inventing with the body in Chaucer's Miller's Tale', in Jeffrey Jerome Cohen and Bonnie Wheeler (eds), *Becoming Male in the Middle Ages*. London and New York: Garland Publishing Inc., 245–60. This interesting article explores the confusion of gender and sexed bodies through the episode of the misdirected kiss in the *Miller's Tale*.

Butler, Judith (1990), *Gender Trouble and the Subversion of Identity*. London and New York: Routledge. See this volume, plus a collection of her essays (2004), in *Undoing Gender*. London and New York: Routledge.

Cohen, Jeffrey Jerome (1999), *Of Giants: Sex, Monsters and the Middle Ages*. Minneapolis, MN: University of Minnesota Press. This book explores the role of the ambiguously gendered giant in a selection of romance tales that includes *Sir Thopas*.

Dinshaw, Carolyn (1995), 'Chaucer's Queer Touches/A Queer Touches Chaucer', in *Exemplaria*, 7.1, 79–97. This groundbreaking article reconsiders the figure of the Pardoner from a queer perspective.

Kruger, Steven (1994), 'Claiming the Pardoner: toward a gay reading of Chaucer's "Pardoner's Tale"', in *Exemplaria*, 6.1 (Spring 1994), 115–40. Kruger offers a close reading of the Pardoner to argue that his figure is a keynote one in gay history.

Lochrie, Karma (1994), 'Women's "pryvetees" and fabliau politics in the *Miller's Tale*', in *Exemplaria*, 6.2, 287–304. This article explores the gender confusion at the heart of the tale and examines the ways in which secrets about women and their bodies circulate amongst men as a means of deflecting anxieties about their own masculinity.

McAlpine, Monica (1980), 'The Pardoner's Homosexuality and How it Matters', in *PMLA*, 95, 8–22. This early essay on the Pardoner considers his ambiguous portrait and argues for its deliberately open-ended nature.

Mcgerr, Rosemarie (1998), *Chaucer's Open Books: Resistance to Closure in Medieval Discourse*. Gainesville, FL: University Press of Florida.

Shoaf, Richard Allen (2001), *Chaucer's Body: The Anxiety of Circulation in The Canterbury Tales*. Gainesville, FL: University Press of Florida. Shoaf offers some rich and provocative readings on a number of the *Tales*.

Sturges, Robert (2000), *Chaucer's Pardoner and Gender Theory: Bodies of Discourse*. New York: Palgrave Macmillan. This studies the Pardoner through a complex range of gender theories. It proves highly useful as a round-up of some key ideas in gender. See also his 'The Pardoner, Veiled and Unveiled' (2000), in Jeffrey Jerome Cohen and Bonnie Wheeler (eds), *Becoming Male in the Middle Ages*, 261–78.

Weisl, Angela Jane (1995), *Conquering the Reign of Femeny*. Cambridge: D. S. Brewer. This consideration of Chaucer's romance tales through the lens of gender theory has important chapters on the *Knight's Tale*, the Wife of Bath and *Sir Thopas*.

4. CRITICAL RECEPTION AND PUBLISHING HISTORY

Essay Collections and General Editions

Ashton, Gail (1998), 'Analysing Texts', in *Chaucer: 'The Canterbury Tales'*. Basingstoke: Macmillan. This is a good introduction with some close critical reading of many of Chaucer's *Tales*, and of some keynote critics, though it needs updating.

Allen, Valerie and Ares Axiotis (eds) (1997), in *Chaucer*, 'New Casebooks'. Basingstoke: Macmillan. This is a good, basic introduction to a selection of critical essays, though you should also read something more up to date.

Ellis, Steve (ed.) (1998), *Chaucer: The 'Canterbury Tales'*, 'Longman Critical Readers'. Harlow: Longman. This is an excellent collection of essays and a clear introduction to some challenging theoretical material.

—— (ed.) (2005), *Chaucer, An Oxford Guide*. Oxford: Oxford University Press. This key volume has a section devoted to a range of new critical readings on several familiar tales from a variety of scholars and perspectives. See the following: Gail Ashton, 'Feminisms', 369–83; Glenn Burger, 'Queer Theory', 432–47; Jeffrey Jerome Cohen, 'Postcolonialism', 448–62; Sylvia Federico, 'New Historicism', 416–31; Patricia Clare Ingham, 'Psychoanalytical Criticism', 463–78; Elizabeth Robertson, 'Modern Chaucer Criticism', 3 55–68; Marion Turner, 'The Carnivalesque', 3 84–99; Barry Windeatt, 'Postmodernism', 400–15.

Phillips, Helen (2000), *An Introduction to the Canterbury Tales: Reading, Fiction, and Context*. Basingstoke: Macmillan. This is an orthodox and comprehensive survey of the *Tales*, useful for quick summaries and the context of works, including sources and analogues.

Earlier Keynote Works

Donaldson, E. Talbot (1970), *Speaking of Chaucer*. London: Athlone Press. Donaldson usefully distinguishes between Chaucer and Chaucer-the-pilgrim narrator. He does this by famously asserting Chaucer's irony, a distance produced by tensions and gaps between a naïve narrator and a moralizing author, a reading that has had a stranglehold on Chaucer Studies for a long time.

Lyman Kittredge, George (1915), *Chaucer and His Poetry*. Cambridge, MA: Harvard University Press.

Robertson, D. W., Jnr (1962), *A Preface to Chaucer*. Princeton, NJ: Princeton University Press.

Postmodern and Psychoanalytical Critical Works

Aranye Fradenburg, Louise O. (2002), *Sacrifice Your Love: Psychoanalysis, Historicism, Chaucer*. Minneapolis, MN: University of Minnesota Press. This challenging read explores

Chaucer from a theoretical perspective, based on the idea of pleasure and desire inherent in sacrifice.

Marshall Leicester, H., Jnr (1990), *The Disenchanted Self: Representing the Subject in the 'Canterbury Tales'*. Berkeley, CA: University of California Press.

Marxist and New Historicist Critical Works
Aers, David (1986), *Chaucer*. Brighton: The Harvester Press.

Patterson, Lee (1991), *Chaucer and the Subject of History*. Madison, WI: University of Wisconsin Press.

Strohm, Paul (1989), *Social Chaucer*. Cambridge, MA: Harvard University Press.

—— (1992), *Hochon's Arrow: The Social Imagination of Fourteenth Century Texts*. Princeton, NJ: Princeton University Press. This examines the connections between Chaucer's works, that of his contemporaries and other historical and legal documents.

Feminist, Gender and Queer Critical Works
Burger, Glenn and Steven F. Kruger (eds) (2001), *Queering the Middle Ages*. Minneapolis, MN: University of Minnesota Press. This collection re-examines the Middle Ages in the light of its sexualities. It has some essays on Chaucer.

Cox, Catherine (1997), *Gender and Language in Chaucer*. Gainesville, FL: University of Florida Press. This is a difficult but interesting exploration of gender. It touches on a variety of tales including the Wife of Bath.

Dinshaw, Carolyn (1989), *Chaucer's Sexual Poetics*. Madison, WI: University of Wisconsin Press.

—— (1999), *Getting Medieval: Sexualities and Communties, Pre- and Postmodern*. Durham, NC: Duke University Press. This key work examines the ways in which notions of sexuality and community are linked, as well how 'history' and historicization is conceived for us.

Hansen, Elaine Tuttle (1992), *Chaucer and the Fictions of Gender*. Berkeley, CA: University of California Press.

Lochrie, Karma (1999), *Covert Operations: The Medieval Uses of Secrecy*. Philadelphia, PA: University of Pennsylvania

Press. Lochrie's stimulating work looks at how medieval sexuality is different from contemporary heterosexuality. The book is also useful for a discussion of a medieval understanding of sodomy and its impact upon ideas about sexuality.

Postcolonial and Nationhood Critical Works

Cohen, Jeffrey Jerome (ed.) (2000), *The Postcolonial Middle Ages*. New York: Palgrave Macmillan. This excellent essay collection has a strong theoretical base.

Ingham, Patricia Clare and Michelle R. Warren (eds) (2003), *Postcolonial Moves: Medieval through Modern*. New York: Palgrave Macmillan. This collection explores postcolonial perspectives, past and present, on Chaucer.

Lynch, Kathryn L. (ed.) (2002), *Chaucer's Cultural Geography*. New York: Routledge. Lynch collates old and new material on Chaucer's place in the context of cultural difference.

5. AFTERLIVES

Andrew, Malcolm (2005), 'Translations', in Ellis (ed.), *Chaucer: An Oxford Guide*, 544–58.

Bowers, John (ed.) (1992), *The Canterbury Tales: Fifteenth-Century Continuations and Additions*. Kalamazoo, MI: Medieval Institute Publications. This compiles, annotates and translates some of Chaucer's spurious material.

Brown, Peter (2005), 'Chaucer and his Guides', in Ellis (ed.), *Chaucer: An Oxford Guide*, 576–90.

Collette, Carolyn (2002), 'Afterlife', in Brown (ed.), *A Companion to Chaucer*, 8–22.

Ellis, Roger (2002), 'Translation', in Brown (ed.), *A Companion to Chaucer*, 443–58.

Ellis, Steve (2000), *Chaucer at Large: The Poet in the Modern Imagination*. Minneapolis, MN: University of Minnesota Press. This is a comprehensive and easy-to-read study of the various Chaucers in evidence in non-academic and popular cultures, past and present. It includes chapters on translation, and Chaucer in performance, among many others.

Forni, Kathleen (2001), *The Chaucerian Apocrypha: A Counterfeit Canon*. Gainesville, FL: University Press of Florida.

Harty, Kevin J. (2005), 'Chaucer in Performance', in Ellis (ed.), *Chaucer: An Oxford Guide*, 560–74.

Matthews, David (2005), 'Reception: eighteenth to nineteenth centuries', in Ellis (ed.), *Chaucer: An Oxford Guide*, 512–25.

Thompson, John J. (2005), 'Reception: fifteenth to seventeenth centuries', in Ellis (ed.), *Chaucer: An Oxford Guide*, 497–509.

Trigg, Stephanie (2002), *Congenial Souls: Reading Chaucer from Medieval to Postmodern*. Minneapolis, MN: University of Minnesota Press. This examines how readers have responded to Chaucer from the fifteenth century to the present day. It includes discussion of a variety of approaches from Virginia Woolf, for example, to contemporary study guides.

— (2005), 'Reception: twentieth and twenty-first centuries,' in Ellis (ed.), *Chaucer: An Oxford Guide*, 528–42.

6. SELECT WEBOGRAPHY

Pointers for using the internet:

- Use internet-related material as supplementary rather than your sole resource. Because the internet is an open-access medium, its status is even less authoritative than printed resources.
- Select sites with care. Sites often replicate select, limited or even erroneous information.
- Remember that sites containing 'edu' or 'ac.uk' in the URL (address) are usually more reputable than commercial or popular pages.
- Remember to update your webography on a regular basis; sites evolve, links may disappear and new information may be added much more quickly than in print format.
- Sometimes URLs refuse access to sites: try Googling the title of the site, or key words, instead.
- For further help in using the internet and to add to the following webography, see Philippa Semper (2005), 'Electronic Resources', in Ellis (ed.), *Chaucer, An Oxford Guide*, 607–17.

Primary Sites
These offer reputable and varied information about Chaucer in different ways. Most are also either metapages or portals. This means they contain links and doorways into other sites and/or review other web pages, thus helping to refine your search.

geoffreychaucer.org
http://geoffreychaucer.org
This is an accessible and non-commercial site with much information and a range of resources. It also offers material on newer or less well-known areas of Chaucer Studies and sets of images to help you reconstruct a medieval context for your reading. If you add the word 'outlines' to the end of the URL, you will find summaries of and study guides to selected tales.

Luminarium Geoffrey Chaucer Page
www.luminarium.org/medlit/chaucer.htm
This extensive site has essays, notes, bibliographies and useful contextual material for many of the tales.

The Chaucer MetaPage
www.unc.edu/depts/chaucer
This well-reputed site has many links to other sites which it also reviews in advance. It collates and reviews electronic online texts of the *Tales* and takes you into other research and source areas, like Chaucer's life and times or Chaucer in popular culture.

Baragona's Chaucer Page
http://academics.vmi.edu/english/chaucer.html
This offers a range of resources and bibliographies, plus a bulletin board, glossary and complete text of the *Tales*.

Hanly's Chaucer Scriptorium
www.wsu.edu:8080/~hanly/chaucer/chaucer.html
This site has a range of links to other resources, reference material, bibliographies, images, and information about the medieval world.

The Harvard Geoffrey Chaucer Page
www.courses.fas.harvard.edu/~chaucer
This highly regarded site has just about everything you might wish to know about Chaucer: bibliographies, translations, essays, contextual and background material. The essays are especially good; they are often short, and new pieces of work rather than replications of existing work.

Dan Kline's The Chaucer Pedagogy Page
http://afdtk.uaa.alaska.edu/pedagogy.htm
This reputable and full site has portals to others of interest, plus a wealth of information of its own, ranging from electronic versions of manuscripts in both Middle and modernized English to essays and contextual material.

ORB: The Online Reference Book for Medieval Studies
www.the-orb.net/encyclop/culture/lit/chaucer.html
This is an academic guide to online resources with original essays, primary sources and material, bibliographies, contextual information and links to other sites.

Electronic Texts
Many of these are illustrated, while some are interactive with audio-visual aids. Most offer modern translations too.

The Electronic Canterbury Tales
www.kankedort.net

Geoffrey Chaucer: Canterbury Tales
http://faculty.acu.edu/-appleton/mbl_fct.htm

Caxton's Canterbury Tales: The British Library Copies
www.cta.dmu.ac.uk/Caxtons
This has copies of the text from 1476 and 1483 in digitized manuscript form, with glosses and hyperlinks. As such, it perhaps comes closest to replicating the reading experiences of medieval audiences to date. Alternatively, go to www.bl.uk/treasures/caxton/homepage.html

The Middle English Collection
http://etext.lib.virginia.edu/collections/languages/english/miden
g/browse.html

The Electronic Literature Foundation: The Canterbury Tales
www.canterburytales.org/canterbury_tales.html
This is an electronic presentation of the poem in several editions
and forms. It has a translation tool with the option to display the
Middle English text alongside a modernization.

Schwartz Memorial Library: Ellesmere Text
www.liu.edu/cwis/cwp/library/sc/chaucer/chaucer.htm
Here you can access images and additional information on the
manuscript that forms the basis of most of our editions of the *Tales*.

Language
University of Wisconsin
www.uwm.edu/Library/special/exhibits/clastext/clspg 073.htm
This has leaves from manuscripts including Caxton's early press of
the poem and a pronunciation guide to Chaucer's Middle English.

Chaucer MetaPage Audio Files
http://academics.vmi.edu/english/audio/audio_index.html

Edwin Duncan's Web Pages
http://towson.edu/~duncan/glossary.html
This site has information about Chaucer's vocabulary and a basic
glossary to help your own reading.

Other Useful Sites
The BBC *Tales* (2003) Online
www.bbc.co.uk/drama/canterburytales/
Though not an academic site, this has a wealth of material and
access to the 2003 BBC TV adaptations of six of the *Tales*.

The Royal Shakespeare Company
This site contains useful learning resources to accompany their
2005 productions of the *Tales*.

www.rsc.org.uk/downloads/learning/rsc_ct_2005_background.pdf
To access interviews with the Directors and Assistant Directors,
go to www.rsc.org.uk/content/3373.aspx
Replace the last part of the URL with '3374.aspx' and '3375.aspx'
to see the full range of material.

The Chaucer Review
www.baylor.edu/~Chaucer-Bibliography
This takes you to an annotated bibliography of the keynote
journal *The Chaucer Review* with a wealth of academic essays,
volumes 1–30 only. For direct access to all of the essays, including more recent ones, go to J-Stor on http://muse.jhu.edu/jour-
nals/cr

The New Chaucer Society
www.ohiostatepress.org
This large and highly influential site has bibliographies, annotations and critical material on Chaucer, as well as volumes to the
keynote journal *Studies in the Age of Chaucer*.

Labyrinth Scholarly Publications
www.georgetown.edu/labyrinth/professional/pubs/scholarly_pu
bs.html
This has easy to navigate links to a variety of online journals.

INDEX